D0041656

The Proven Method for Building Strategy, Focusing Your Resources, and Taking Smart Action

RICH HORWATH

Greenleaf Book Group Press

Published by Greenleaf Book Group Press
Austin, Texas
www.greenleafbookgroup.com

Distributed by Greenleaf Book Group LLC

For ordering information or special discounts for bulk purchases, please contact Greenleaf Book Group LLC at PO Box 91869, Austin, TX 78709, 512.891.6100.

Design and composition by Greenleaf Book Group LLC
Cover design by Greenleaf Book Group LLC

Publisher's Cataloging-In-Publication Data
(Prepared by The Donohue Group, Inc.)

Horwath, Rich.

Deep dive : the proven method for building strategy, focusing your resources, and taking smart action /¬ Rich Horwath. -- 1st ed.

p. : ill., charts ; cm.

Includes index.

ISBN: 978-1-929774-82-1

1. Strategic planning. 2. Business planning. I. Title.

HD30.28 .H679 2009

658.4/01 2009925203

Part of the Tree Neutral™ program, which offsets the number of trees consumed in the production and printing of this book by taking proactive steps, such as planting trees in direct proportion to the number of trees used: www.treeneutral.com

Printed in the United States of America on acid-free paper

09 10 11 12 13 14 10 9 8 7 6 5 4 3 2 1

Second Edition

For my wife, Anne,

who makes Wonder Woman look like a slacker

CONTENTS

ACKNOWLEDGMENTS

I'd like to thank my wife, Anne, for her strength, compassion, and optimistic attitude, all of which have nurtured a wonderful family. Thanks to my children, Luke and Jessica, for filling our home with love and laughter. I am eternally grateful to my parents, Jan and Rich, and sister, Sharon, for blessing me with their love and thoughtfulness and providing the ultimate role model for a happy family.

I'd also like to thank the following business leaders for providing me with their wisdom and experiences through our work together: Mark Sutter, Don Pogorzelski, Jerry Casey, Bob Schruender, Allan Murphy, Paul O'Connor, Norman Tashash, Chris Anderson, Nilaksh Kothari, Andrew de Guttadauro, Dean Gregory, Sharon Ryan, Dan Linden, Rob Schneider, Phil Tegeler, Bob Palumbo, Craig Besler, Marti Hayes, Michael Mehler, Rob Paterkiewicz, Jeffrey Sanfilippo, Jasper Sanfilippo Jr., Mike Valentine, Tom Fordonski, Domenick DiCindio, Terry Walsh, Kathy Billings, and Robert Hanf.

Thanks to the leadership team at the Lake Forest Graduate School of Management, especially Arlene Mayzel and Frank Brletich. Their guidance and friendship have helped me develop my teaching skills and given me the opportunity to educate a wonderful group of students. I am also very grateful to the students at LFGSM who have helped me continue to grow through our dynamic and insightful class discussions.

Finally, a special thanks to the amazing team at Greenleaf Book Group for their wonderful work throughout the publishing process, especially Chris McRay, Kristen Sears, Tanya Hall, Lisa Woods, Jay Hodges, Jeanne Pinault, Carrie Winsett, and Linda O'Doughda.

CHAPTER 1

HOW DEEP CAN YOU DIVE?

> Be not the slave of your own past. Plunge into the sublime seas, dive deep and swim far, so you shall come back with self-respect, with new power, with an advanced experience that shall explain and overlook the old.
>
> **—Ralph Waldo Emerson, writer and philosopher**

Immersed in the sea of crystal blue water, I checked the tank's pressure gauge and verified what I had just noted. I was out of air. Unable to take another breath from the tank, I quickly ascended until my scuba mask crashed through the surface of the water into the warm Caribbean breeze. Yanking the regulator from my lips, I gulped in a huge mouthful of life-sustaining air. I then put in my snorkel and swam to shore. My inability to breathe had provided me with a forceful reminder of the importance of intelligently using one's limited resources—in this case, oxygen.

And so it is with strategy. Each day we rely on strategy to determine how we use our limited resources to better our organization's place in the competitive landscape. Many firms never get to the point of "taking their last breaths," and so they continue to slowly leak resources that dooms them to mediocre existences. It seems that without the watchful eye of urgency, the discipline to intelligently allocate our resources—time talent, and money—is washed out with the receding tide.

All managers have these resources to varying degrees within their organizations, and they must decide how to manage each. So, technically, all managers are strategists. The reality, however, is that not all managers are good strategists. Herein lies the pearl of great opportunity: the deeper you can dive into the business and resurface with strategic insights, the more valuable you'll become to your organization. Effective resource allocation drives profitability (more resources invested in the right activities) and productivity (fewer resources invested in the wrong activities). The result is a high-performance organization in which all levels of management are encouraged and equipped to shape its strategic direction.

ARE YOU STRATEGIC?

I was thrown out of college for cheating
on the metaphysics exam; I looked into
the soul of the boy sitting next to me.

—Woody Allen, writer, director, and actor

Until now, looking into someone's soul was about the only way we've had to guess whether or not someone is "strategic." In many organizations it is assumed that senior executives are strategic and lower-level employees are not. As you might imagine, solely using someone's title to determine his or her strategic ability is as accurate as using a Hollywood star's popularity to determine his or her knowledge of political issues.

Research on leadership by the American Management Association has shown that the most important competency for a leader is the ability to develop strategy.[1] Unfortunately, when researchers examined leaders at all levels in organizations, they found only 4 percent to be strategists.[2] According to the Institute of Directors in London, the wide gap between the importance of strategic thinking and the percentage of leaders who actually are strategic can be attributed to the fact that 90 percent of executives at the director and vice president levels have had no training to become competent strategists.[3] Organizations tend to invest training and development resources in the tangible operational areas of sales, customer service, and communication while neglecting the critical area of strategic thinking. Consider your organization. When was the last time you and your colleagues were provided with developmental programs specifically geared toward strategic thinking?

TIME TROUBLE

The worst enemy of the strategist is the clock.
Time trouble, as we call it in chess, reduces us
all to pure reflex and reaction, tactical play.

—Garry Kasparov, former world chess champion

We all know the popular maxim that the most precious commodity is time. Time is the one resource that can't be renewed. Entire industries have been built around providing people with more time by outsourcing the less desirable tasks that can eat away at it: for example, cleaning services, lawn maintenance, and concierge-type services. Most of the ramifications of a lack of strategic thinking relate to wasting time. What follows are just a few examples from recent research:

- "Our research suggests that 85 percent of executive leadership teams spend less than one hour per month discussing their unit's strategy, with 50 percent spending no time at all."[4]

- "Our findings on managerial behavior should frighten you: Fully 90 percent of managers squander their time in all sorts of ineffective activities. In other words, a mere 10 percent of managers spend their time in a committed, purposeful and reflective manner."[5]
- "Eighty percent of top management's time is devoted to issues that account for less than 20 percent of [a] company's long-term value."[6]
- "The main problem identified by the majority of senior executives was strategic thinking. 'Our senior executives tend to get carried away by details and lose their strategic perspective. It is a major challenge to get our decision makers to think in strategic, rather than operational, terms.'"[7]

A lack of strategic thinking not only prevents individual managers from maximizing the critical resource of time but also can stop the entire firm's progress in its tracks. A study was conducted of five hundred companies to better understand what causes successful organizations to struggle financially for extended periods of time. The researchers found that 87 percent of these companies suffered one or more "stall points," a term for the start of a prolonged financial decline. The effects of these stall points can be devastating. The study further reported that "On average, companies lose 74 percent of their market capitalization as measured against the S&P 500 index in the decade surrounding a growth stall."[8]

When the researchers pored through data to uncover the cause of stall points, they found that 70 percent were attributed to poor choices about strategy. While it's convenient to blame the economy for one's misfortunes, the data clearly show that most financial decline is well within management's control. Today, the reality is that battles in business are waged with one weapon—the mind. How sharp is yours?

Academicians and executives alike echo the urgency of improving strategic thinking skills. Just listen to the following thought-leader comments:

- "There are no substitutes for strategic thinking. Improving quality is meaningless without knowing what kind of quality is relevant in competitive terms."[9]
- "The ability to think and plan strategically for the future is the most important single skill of effective executives."[10]
- "Although companies find it difficult to change strategy for many reasons, one stands out: strategic thinking is not a core managerial competence at most companies."[11]
- "At the speed of business today, it's essential to turn technical pro's (e.g., engineers, scientists, clinicians) into strategic thinkers who grasp a company's core functions."[12]
- "In the environment we're in, good execution and good operations aren't enough to fix a business with a flawed strategy. So you need to spend time understanding what businesses you think you are going to work, what business models seem to make sense. Strategy is more important than ever before."[13]

If we heed the advice of these thought-leaders about the critical need for enhanced strategic thinking, exactly how do we get there? After all, strategy is an abstract concept we can't just reach out and touch, and that makes the process of thinking about it much more difficult. We can begin by defining strategic thinking as the generation and application of business insights on a continual basis to achieve competitive advantage.

Strategic thinking is the generation and application of business insights on a continual basis to achieve competitive advantage.

Just as intelligent allocation of limited resources is at the heart of strategy, insight is at the heart of strategic thinking. Insight is the difference between taking a business-as-usual incremental approach and pursuing dynamic game-changing initiatives that separate winners from losers. Too often in the "action is everything" world we live in, we are hamsters running on a wheel. Day in and day out, we run faster and faster, doing the same things in the same ways we've always done them. Trouble is, we're often doing the wrong things: things that drain critical resources from those few effective tasks that really will make us successful. If we think of our business as a Ferrari and strategy as the steering wheel, insights are the key to the ignition. A business without insights is like a Ferrari without the key: it looks sensational on the outside, but it isn't going anywhere.

Insights also act as the bridge between experience and expertise. Take the United States Postal Service, for example. It has been in business since 1789, which means it has 220 years of experience delivering things. It also happens to misdirect, damage, and lose numerous items each year. FedEx, on the other hand, has been in business for just 38 years, yet it has revolutionized the industry, becoming the most versatile mover of goods in the world, with on-time delivery rates of 99.8 percent!

Experience without expertise means nothing. Just because someone has forty years of experience breathing doesn't necessarily mean they're getting better at it. And unless you are actively generating *insights* about your business on a continual basis, you are

DIVE MASTER PRACTICE

How do you generate new insights about your business? What insight-generating tools do you use? Where do you keep track of your insights on a regular basis? What are the three most important insights you've learned during the past month?

simply not taking full advantage of your experience. Insights are the bridge connecting experience to expertise, and strategic thinking is how we build that bridge of insights every day we're in business.

As we saw in the USPS example, experience alone can be a very deceptive predictor of success. This is often apparent in the importance placed on experience in the hiring process. While experience is often touted as the best indicator that a candidate will be successful, in fact, eighty years of data show that experience is only the *fifth* best predictor of job success.[14]

For example, several years ago three vice chairmen were vying for the CEO position at Pfizer—the largest pharmaceutical company in the world. Two of the candidates each had more than thirty-five years of pharmaceutical industry experience, while the third had only four within that industry. Yet the board chose Jeffrey Kindler, a lawyer with just four years of pharmaceutical experience. Of Kindler's selection, Pfizer board member Stanley Ikenberry says: "We had a general feeling that the external environment for pharmaceutical companies is changing rapidly. Jeff is a very strategic thinker."[15]

Think of experience like cholesterol: there is the good kind and the bad kind. Active experience is the good cholesterol (HDL); passive experience is the bad cholesterol (LDL). Active experience involves continually taking on challenges that are just outside your competence or current ability level. Active experience means monitoring your progress and generating insights as to how to close the gap between where you are and where you want to be.

In contrast, passive experience involves going through the motions of the activity with no focus on concrete steps for improving performance. It means charging through each day without ever stopping to gain the insights from your efforts. Think of all the sales reps, marketing managers, senior executives, church choirs, and weekend golfers who pile up years of experience without ever getting better. The price you pay for not transforming passive experience into active experience is obsolescence. As author David Mayer writes, "When emphasis is placed on experience and experience counts more than such essentials as empathy and drive, what is accomplished can only be called the inbreeding of mediocrity."[16] Don't be discouraged, however. There is a bridge above the perilous waters of obsolescence that can take you from passive experience to expertise. That bridge is insight.

The Nobel Prize–winning German economist Reinhard Selten describes that bridge in this way: "I run business decision-making experiments both with experienced managers and with university students. Overall, the students do much better. It's always the same story: People are guided too much by little-understood experience and make the wrong generalizations. Less experience can be advantageous when it forces you to think harder."[17]

The natural reaction of managers with twenty-plus years of experience in their fields is to dismiss these data as not real world. But look again at Selten's comment that "People are guided too much by little-understood experience" and it begins to make sense. If time isn't invested in strategic thinking—that is, in generating insights about experience—then that experience is indeed being wasted. It's certainly not being transformed into expertise. As Gus Pagonis, former head of logistics for the U.S. Army, says, "I can think of no leader, military or business, who has achieved success in his or her position without some profound expertise."[18]

Albert Einstein defined insanity as doing the same thing over and over and expecting different results. Insanity in business is using the same assumptions and outdated tactics year after year and expecting dramatically *better* results. Yet, isn't that what most of us do? Companies continually forecast sizeable increases in revenue and sales without providing their teams with new ways to think about the business and generate insights. A simple but often-overlooked premise in business is that *new growth comes from new thinking.*

Expecting new growth without new ways—concepts, tools, and frameworks—to think about the business is like a farmer expecting to grow new crops without first planting the seeds. For anyone under the impression that working harder at doing the same things in the same ways will generate new growth, please hop into a time machine and transport yourself back to 1960. It is crucial that everyone—especially those who have their heads buried in the sand of business by busyness—identify new ways to think about their work.

The Chinese philosopher Chuang Tzu wrote: "When people wish to see their reflections, they do not look into running water; they look into still water. Only that which is still can hold other things still." Taking time to reflect and evaluate why we're doing what we're doing and how to become more effective will both provide answers and evoke deeper questions. Sure, we can continue to use a blizzard of activity as an analgesic, numbing us to the pain of knowing we're potentially wasting our time and talent in the wrong activities, the wrong work, the wrong job, the wrong company, or maybe even the wrong vocation. Or we can stop and look into the still water and find out what's really there, and then make some important changes in our work and in our lives.

The ability of executives to think strategically has the most relevance in today's dynamic business environment. Strategic thinking (defined, remember, as the generation and application of business insights on a continual basis to achieve competitive advantage) is different from strategic planning. We can define strategic planning as the channeling of insights into an action plan to achieve goals and objectives. A key distinction between strategic thinking and strategic planning is that the former occurs on a regular basis, as part of our daily activities, while the latter usually occurs annually. One of the reasons management scholars such as Henry Mintzberg of McGill University and Richard Rumelt of UCLA have lampooned strategic planning is that in many cases, it is an annual pilgrimage disguising the inherent flaws in the process. Professor Rumelt says:

"Most corporate strategic plans have little to do with strategy. They are simply three-year or five-year rolling resource budgets and some sort of market share projection. Calling this strategic planning creates false expectations that the exercise will somehow produce a coherent strategy."[19]

Unlike the additional work that is created by the process of strategic planning, we can understand strategic thinking as using a new lens to view all aspects of the business at all times. It's not about *adding* more work. It's about *enhancing* the view of the work and improving one's ability to perform it. As professor Mintzberg puts it: "Strategic planning is not strategic thinking. Indeed, strategic planning often spoils strategic thinking, causing managers to confuse real vision with the manipulation of numbers."[20]

Over time, strategic planning has erroneously become the umbrella for strategy development. Strategy development consists of a five-phase process, from discovery through implementation; strategic planning is merely one of those five phases. As such, strategic planning is therefore an event that occurs on a periodic basis. Strategic thinking, on the other hand, is an ongoing mind-set that can be developed by practicing its three disciplines—which I introduce toward the end of this chapter—and by continually seeking the insights into your company that lead to competitive advantage.

THE FOUR TYPES OF STRATEGIC THINKERS

You've likely noticed during your daily encounters with bosses, colleagues, direct reports, customers, suppliers, and other individuals that strategic thinking comes in varying degrees, ranging from brilliant to nonexistent. To help you refine your idea of strategic thinking, I have taken the results of research I conducted among senior managers from 154 companies and have identified four types of strategic thinkers. These will help you better understand how to think strategically and will give you insight into individuals in your organization. Two criteria to consider as you evaluate an individual's ability to provide strategic insight are what I call the "Impact of Insights" and the "Frequency of Insights."

I use the analogy of underwater diving to explain the types of strategic thinkers I've researched. Just as there are four types of divers, so too are there four types of strategic thinkers (as shown in Figure 1.1).

1. **Beach Bums**: They sit on the shore and make no attempt to enter the water. This type of manager doesn't contribute insight into the business. The research shows, on average, that 9 percent of managers are Beach Bums.
2. **Snorkelers**: They swim on the surface of the water, equipped with a diving mask and swim fins. This type of manager offers tactical solutions to issues, but the solutions don't have a significant positive impact on the business. As

Figure 1.1 The Four Types of Strategic Thinkers

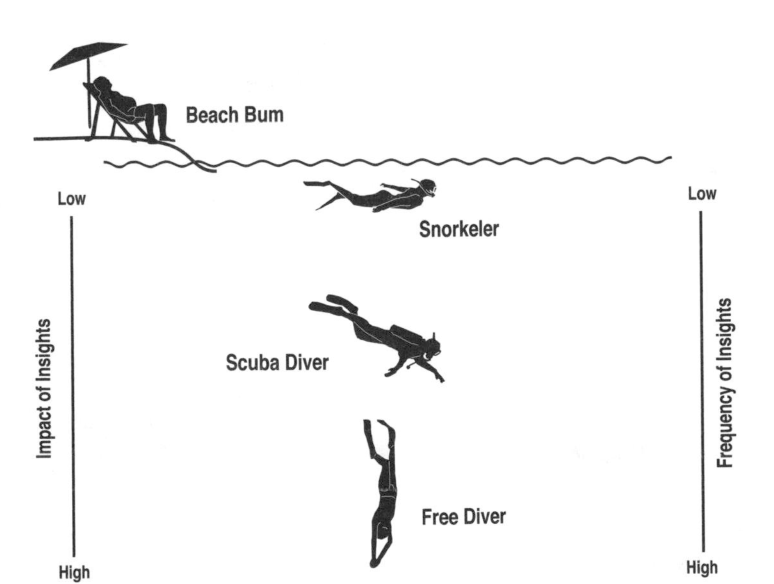

the name indicates, they tend to do surface thinking and seldom get to the heart of an issue. Research indicates, on average, that 26 percent of managers are Snorkelers.

3. **Scuba Divers**: They swim underwater wearing a diving mask, swim fins, a wetsuit, and a portable apparatus containing compressed air. This type of manager can produce strategic insights for solutions but requires instruction and assistance to do so. These managers can provide ideas that advance the overall success of the business, but they need a setting such as a group strategic planning meeting to contribute. When these managers are thoroughly prepared with the proper data and market research prior to a meeting, and are then led through the meeting with frameworks and models, they can generate highly effective insights. However, because they generate insights only when heavily equipped, the insights are infrequent and tend to occur only in a meeting environment. Study results show, on average, that 32 percent of managers can be classified as Scuba Divers.
4. **Free Divers**: They dive underwater without the assistance of a portable breathing apparatus in an attempt to attain great depths. This is the type of strategic thinker leaders aspire to be. These managers generate effective insights about the business on a regular basis. Although they use a customary portfolio of questions, frameworks, and models to guide their thinking, they are able to summon the appropriate tool and combine it with the right data to continually generate insights that transform the business. The research indicates that, on average, only three of every ten managers are Free Divers (see Figure 1.2).

At first blush, it would appear that the only things standing in a manager's way of becoming a Free Diver are adequate knowledge

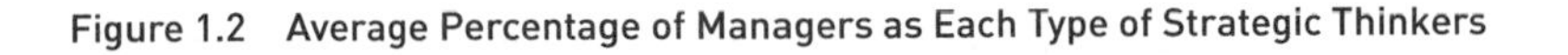

Figure 1.2 Average Percentage of Managers as Each Type of Strategic Thinkers

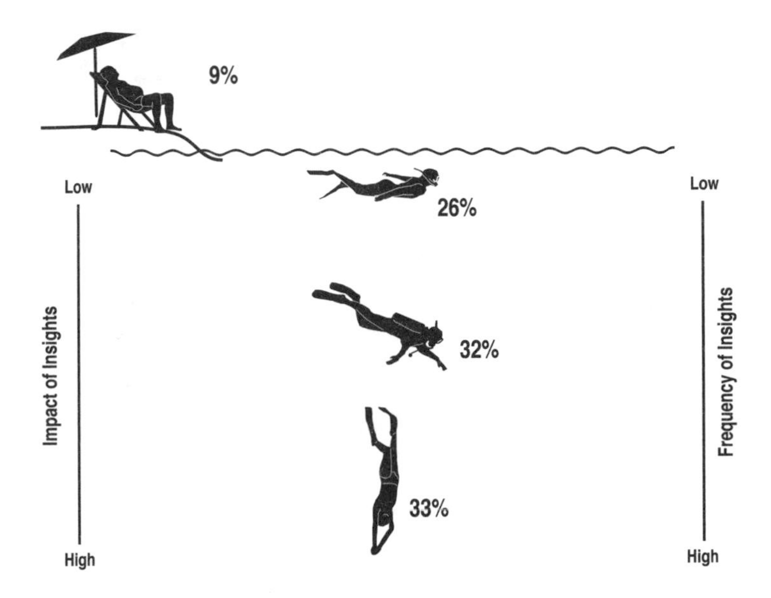

and mental models to think strategically on a regular basis. While these do account for a large portion of the cases, a subtler reason also exists. Strategic thinking, and the actions taken to follow through on it, requires an appetite for risk. Strategy calls for focus and the trade-offs that inherently follow, but many managers decide they would rather play it safe. In most organizations, sins of commission—taking a risk and failing—are punished much more harshly than sins of omission—not taking a risk and missing out on a great opportunity. With both political (your reputation within the company) and career (not wanting to jeopardize your next promotion) ramifications to consider, many managers consciously opt out of strategic thinking. And that is a shame. As Roberto Goizueta, the successful former CEO of Coca-Cola, points out: "If you take risks, you may still fail. If you do not take risks, you will surely fail. The greatest risk of all is to do nothing."

DIVE MASTER PRACTICE

Consider your daily activities. How often do you have the opportunity to come up with insights that change the course of your work? What level of effect do those insights have on your business? What type of strategic thinker are you currently—a Beach Bum, a Snorkeler, a Scuba Diver, or a Free Diver? Consider your colleagues in the department. What percentage are Beach Bums? Snorkelers? Scuba Divers? Free Divers?

THE STRATEGIC THINKING ASSESSMENT

If a management team is willing to take calculated risks and is intent on becoming more effective strategists, a first step is to assess their baseline strategic thinking skills. As the old medical adage goes, prescription without diagnosis equals malpractice. You wouldn't trust a physician who walked into the exam room where you were waiting, took one look at you, and wrote a prescription without asking any questions. By the same token, asking questions to assess your team's baseline strategic thinking skills is an important starting point.

I developed the Strategic Thinking Assessment as an objective way to evaluate a manager's strategic thinking skills by using a list of fifty questions. The questions are grouped under ten strategic thinking skills (see Figure 1.3), five questions per skill.

A brief explanation of the ten strategic thinking skills follows:

1. Strategy: mastering the three criteria of great strategy (acumen, allocation, and action—which I describe in detail later in the chapter)

Figure 1.3 Ten Strategic Thinking Skills

2. Insight: generating new ideas about the business
3. Context: understanding the current situation
4. Competitive Advantage: creating distinct offerings with superior value
5. Value: determining the benefits/costs of the offerings
6. Resource Allocation: deciding where to focus capital, talent, and time
7. Modeling: visually capturing the essence of business issues
8. Innovation: creating new value for customers
9. Purpose: developing mission, vision, and values
10. Mental Agility: the ability to improvise, adapt, and excel through adversity

The Strategic Thinking Assessment has been administered to hundreds of executives around the world to shed light on their individual thinking skills and the level of support they receive from their organizations in their efforts to think strategically. At the writing of this book, the average score is 58 out of 100 points. Considering so few resources have been invested in educating and training managers to become more effective strategists, this low score is not surprising.

The following are sample questions taken from the assessment:

1. Successful business strategy is about:
   A. Being better than the competition.
   B. Having the "right people on the bus."
   C. Being different from the competition.

2. One method of influencing competitive advantage is to:
   A. Reduce prices to drive out competition.
   B. Change the customer's value preferences.
   C. Benchmark competitors and excel at best practices.

3. Context is defined as:
   A. The specific problem in a given business situation.
   B. The circumstances in which an event occurs.
   C. The combination of strengths and weaknesses an organization possesses to balance with opportunities and threats.

4. For my business, purpose in the form of a mission, vision, or values statement:
   A. Influences my daily activities.
   B. Doesn't exist.
   C. In reality has little, if any, effect on my business.

5. The three value disciplines are:
   A. Revenue growth, gross margin, and return on capital.
   B. Customer intimacy, operational excellence, and product leadership.
   C. Operational effectiveness, low-cost leadership, and innovation.

As data from the Strategic Thinking Assessment indicate, there is a big difference between tossing the word *strategic* around in the conference room and knowing what it really means.

THE THREE DISCIPLINES OF STRATEGIC THINKING

Strategic thinking rarely occurs spontaneously.

—Michael Porter, professor, Harvard Business School

By now you know that strategic thinking is the ability to generate and apply insights on a continual basis to achieve competitive advantage. Knowing the definition by itself, however, does not move you closer to practical application. When working with an intangible concept like strategy, it's often helpful to affix it to a more concrete framework. My research indicates that strategic thinking consists of three disciplines (as shown in Figure 1.4):

1. Acumen, which helps you generate key business insights
2. Allocation, which focuses resources through trade-offs
3. Action, which requires executing strategy to achieve goals

These "three As" provide a simple yet comprehensive framework for applying strategic thinking to the real-world business issues you will face. They provide you with the mental strength, agility,

Figure 1.4 Three Disciplines of Strategic Thinking

and confidence you need to successfully traverse the competitive landscape.

You may wonder why I chose the word *discipline* to describe the three As. In an age when it is easy to be swept away by the tidal wave of urgent but unimportant things in the form of e-mails, voicemails, and tactical firefighting, discipline is often the only thing that can keep us on track. Discipline is what makes us ask why. Discipline is what makes us challenge last year's assumptions. And discipline is what prevents us from wasting precious hours, days, and weeks on things that simply don't matter. Study the habits of chess grand masters, classical musicians, and world-class athletes, and the one thing they all have in common is discipline. Strategic thinking is no different. If you want to elevate yourself to the pinnacle of enduring business success, you must master the three disciplines of strategic thinking.

The remainder of this book is devoted to the practical application of the three disciplines of strategic thinking to your business. Prior to the in-depth look at the three disciplines in chapters 3 through 5, I provide an overview of strategy in chapter 2 to create a foundation for understanding this fundamental concept at the core of strategic thinking.

PEARLS OF INSIGHT

- **Strategic thinking is defined as the generation and application of business insights on a continual basis to achieve competitive advantage.**

- **New growth comes from new thinking.**

- **Strategic planning is the channeling of the insights generated by strategic thinking into an action plan to achieve goals and objectives.**

- **There are four types of strategic thinkers:**
  1. Beach Bums are managers who don't contribute insights to the business.
  2. Snorkelers are managers who offer tactical solutions to issues, but their solutions don't have a significant positive impact on the business.
  3. Scuba Divers are managers who can produce strategic insights for solutions, but they require instruction and assistance to do so.
  4. Free Divers are managers who, on a regular basis, generate insights that have a significant impact on the business.

- **There are ten strategic thinking skills:**
    1. Strategy: mastering the three criteria of great strategy
    2. Insight: generating new ideas about the business
    3. Context: understanding the current situation
    4. Competitive Advantage: creating distinct offerings with superior value
    5. Value: determining the benefits/costs of the offerings
    6. Resource Allocation: deciding where to focus capital, talent, and time
    7. Modeling: visually capturing the essence of business issues
    8. Innovation: creating new value for customers
    9. Purpose: developing mission, vision, and values
    10. Mental Agility: the ability to improvise, adapt, and excel through adversity

- **There are three disciplines of strategic thinking:**
    1. Acumen, which helps generate key business insights
    2. Allocation, which focuses resources through trade-offs
    3. Action, which requires executing strategy to achieve goals

CHAPTER 2

PREPARING TO DIVE

> All of us have in our veins the exact same percentage of salt in our blood that exists in the ocean, and therefore, we have salt in our blood, in our sweat, in our tears. We are tied to the ocean. And when we go back to the sea—whether it is to sail or to watch it—we are going back [to] whence we came.
>
> **—John F. Kennedy, thirty-fifth president of the United States**

The retirement of Bob Barker, longtime host of the game show *The Price Is Right*, was a dark day for all of us in the world of business strategy. Okay, not really. But imagine for a moment a game show called *What's Your Strategy?* featuring executives from leading companies. Using actual quotations from business publications, the game show might go something like this:

> **Host:** Ladies and gentlemen, please welcome the CEO of Wendy's, Kerrii Anderson. All right, Kerrii, for a lifetime supply of chocolate Frosties, what's your strategy?
>
> **Anderson**: Three key strategies are to strengthen core business, execute new initiatives, and reduce costs.[1]

Buzzzzzz!

Host: I'm sorry, but those aren't strategies, they're goals. Thanks for playing. As a lovely parting gift, we have a Happy Meal from McDonald's. Since they've been eating your lunch, seems only fair you get a little of theirs.

Our next contestant hails from Macy's Department Store, the company that decided to scrap the historic Marshall Field's brand name after the acquisition. Please welcome the former chairman of Macy's North Division, Frank Guzzetta.

Frank, we understand sales have dropped like a rock since you decided to change the brand name of Marshall Field's to Macy's. For the chance to be the Grand Marshal—I mean Macy—of the Thanksgiving Day Parade, what's your strategy?

Guzzetta: We're trying to find the people that were customers and didn't come back. That's a major strategy.[2]

Buzzzzzz!

Host: I'm sorry Frank, but that's not even a minor strategy. It's an aspiration of sorts, but it doesn't even qualify as a vision. As a parting gift you'll receive one box of Marshall Field's—I mean Macy's—famous Frango Mints. Enjoy!

Our final contestant on *What's Your Strategy?* is the former CEO of Pfizer, Hank McKinnell. As you finish your tenure at the world's largest pharmaceutical company, Hank, what's your strategy?

McKinnell: Our strategy is to survive this period, and "survival" is the right word.[3]

Buzzzzzz!

Host: I'm sorry Hank, but survival is the *wrong* word. In fact, saying your strategy is survival when you've been swimming in more resources than most companies could ever dream of is pathetic. We had a lovely parting gift for you—a Viagra coffee mug! But since you received a nearly $200 million severance package while the company's stock price dropped 40 percent during your tenure . . . we're keeping the cup.

That's all for this week's show. Until next week—stay strategic, San Diego!

OBSTACLES TO PRACTICING SOUND STRATEGIC THINKING

As these actual quotes illustrate, even C-level executives at world-renowned companies don't always practice sound strategic thinking. Why? For three reasons: (1) abstraction, (2) differing definitions, and (3) lack of knowledge.

First, strategy is an abstract concept. You can't reach out and touch it. Whenever an abstract concept is involved, there is plenty of room for interpretation. Second, different companies have different definitions of strategy. Different business units within companies have different definitions of strategy. And different groups within those business units have different definitions of strategy. Considering that people often move from company to company, we see how quickly things can get muddled. Third, most organizations pour their training resources into building operational skills—customer service, sales, communications, etc.—putting little, if any, resources toward building the strategy skills of their management teams.

To help clarify strategy, we can use the ABCs of what strategy is not. Strategy is not

- Aspiration: goals, objectives, or visions

- Best practices: trying to be better than, instead of different from, the competition
- Caution: being tentative and restrained, afraid to make trade-offs

Aspiration

Too often, strategy is mistaken for aspiration, and it takes the form of a goal, an objective, or a vision. How often have you seen strategy written as "to be the market leader," or "to grow new business," or "to be the premier provider of . . ."? The "what" you're trying to achieve, whether it be a goal, an objective, or a long-term vision, should never be confused with "how" you will achieve it, which is the strategy.

Best Practices

Best practices can be crucial to success, but they should never be confused with strategy. While they are important for operational areas of an organization, if substituted for strategy, best practices can quickly lead to an erosion of the business. Best practices erode advantage because if more than one company is using a best practice, the necessary differentiation of strategy fades away, and the offerings can begin to look the same in the eyes of the customers. Once the differences among competitors are whittled away, the only thing left for customers to decide on is price.

Caution

Strategy is not caution. If you aren't willing to assume risk, make trade-offs, and upset somebody along the way—including, maybe, even some customers—then you don't have a strategy. Too often managers striving for that next promotion play it safe and spread their resources evenly across the business. This offers the same result as spreading personal finances evenly across all the investment tools—a muted, mediocre performance in the short term that falls significantly behind others willing to focus their resources in the long term. Trade-offs inherently involve risk, and risk means a potential loss of resources, revenue, and, possibly, that next step on the career ladder. Is it any wonder managers are reluctant to make trade-offs?

A study of nearly one thousand executives published in *Strategy Magazine* showed that 50 percent of the respondents felt their senior management teams could neither develop a competent strategy for their organizations nor execute their strategies.[4] Consider these data along with research published in the journal *Long Range Planning*, showing that nearly 40 percent of organizations have no formal process for developing strategy.[5] This would be the same as

- Four of every ten cars on the road operating without a steering wheel.
- Four of every ten pro football teams having no playbook.
- Four of every ten fashion designers being color-blind (although if you've seen ties in a men's store lately, you may think this is already true).

When we add these pieces of research to the "What Strategy Is Not" puzzle, it begins to show why so many organizations continue to be mired in the muck of mediocrity. Remembering the ABCs of what strategy is not—aspiration, best practices, and caution—will help keep your business running smoothly. Otherwise, you may be the next contestant receiving parting gifts in the real-world version of *What's Your Strategy?*

Remember, strategy is *not* aspiration, best practices, or caution.

When we're new parents, we think our children are perfect. That is, of course, until the first time we see them in the sandbox scooping handfuls of sand into their mouths like it was Froot

Loops. Then we realize our definition of "gifted" may be off. When it comes to strategy, organizations are a lot like parents. We tend to think our strategies are perfect too. That is, of course, until a new competitor enters the market and begins chiseling away at our customer base. Then we rush to react, like a bumper car spinning out of control, and find ourselves way off course, wondering how we ever got into this position.

STRATEGY DEFINED

In those times when we're faced with difficult business decisions, it's helpful to get back to strategy's foundation. Business strategy is defined as "the intelligent allocation of limited resources through a unique system of activities to outperform the competition in serving customers."[6]

Resource Allocation

A number of important concepts make up strategy. The first is the intelligent allocation of limited resources. Resources can take the form of the tangible (physical assets and financial resources), the intangible (culture, brand, reputation), and the human (knowledge, competencies, and skills).

When the idea of "limited" resources is introduced, attention immediately goes to the tangible area of resources, as nearly everyone clamors for a larger budget with which to work. A frequently overlooked source of great waste in many organizations is the ineffective allocation of the human resources of time and talent. Many executives are shocked when they track where their time and talent are actually spent each day. In many cases, they slowly leak into activities and meetings that add little, if any, value to the attainment of their primary goals. Companies lose tremendous profits and productivity due to unclear purpose in the form of mission and vision, incongruent strategic direction, and the unwillingness to make trade-offs. The organizations that successfully show employees the link between the purpose of their work and the strategy for achieving their goals unleash their maximum potential. Conducting periodic resource audits is an important first step in determining where profit and productivity improvements can be made. As David Collis and Cynthia Montgomery of Harvard Business School note: "Strategy is a matter of deploying the firm's resource bundle to meet the needs of the marketplace while blunting the ability of rivals to respond effectively. Thus, resources and capabilities lie at the very heart of business-level strategy. Because valuable resources often can be leveraged across the multiple businesses of a diversified firm, they lie at the heart of corporate-level strategy as well."[7]

Unique System of Activities

The second aspect of our definition of business strategy is having a unique system of activities. Nestled in the middle of the definition, this idea of differentiation is perhaps the most overlooked tenet of strategy. Differentiation for competitive advantage in business has its roots in science. In 1934, Moscow University professor G. F. Gause published the results of a landmark study. He placed small animals in a bottle with an ample amount of food. If the animals were of the same genus and a different species, they were able to live together peaceably. However, if the animals were of the same genus and the same species, they were not able to coexist. This led to the Principle of Competitive Exclusion, which states that no two species can coexist that make their living in the identical way.[8]

Open the newspaper and read about the companies that are struggling and it's a good bet one of the reasons is their failure to heed the Principle of Competitive Exclusion. They are stuck doing the same things in the same way as their competition. Jeff Immelt, chairman and CEO of General Electric, understood the importance of differentiation when he wrote, "GE must look different . . .

act different . . . be different . . . to excel in the years ahead."[9] Notice he didn't write that GE must be "better." He specifically chose the word *different* and used it three times to emphasize his company's understanding that the road to business success is paved with differentiation from the competition.

What do the American singer and songwriter Johnny Cash and the Mini Cooper automobile have in common? Johnny Cash didn't have the best singing voice of his era, and the Mini Cooper isn't the highest performance automobile on the market. They have both been remarkably successful, however, not because they were *better* but because they were *different* from their competition in ways their core customers valued.

> Johnny Cash and the Mini Cooper have both been remarkably successful because they were *different* from their competition in ways their core customers valued.

Taking the concept of differentiation in strategy a step further, we can view strategy with two lenses:

1. Performing different activities from the competition
2. Performing similar activities in a different way from the competition

An example of the first lens was the advent of Netflix in 1998. Instead of having a customer go to a store to rent DVDs, Netflix had the customer order DVDs online. Netflix pioneered the online system for renting DVDs delivered by mail, complemented by proprietary software for queuing and recommending movies. Add to that their library of ninety thousand titles, and their differentiated activities have made them a highly competitive player in the DVD market.

Enterprise Rent-A-Car exemplifies the second lens. Enterprise performs the same general activity as its competitors in that it rents automobiles to customers. Enterprise differs in these ways, however: delivering cars to customers; operating in small, inexpensive offices in metro areas; using older, soon-to-be-discontinued cars; and keeping reservations in-house. Enterprise serves as a successful reminder that even though we may perform an activity similar to our competitors, we cannot abdicate our responsibility of digging in to find a unique system of different ways to perform that activity.

Based on these two lenses, strategic leaders are continually asking the following two questions:

1. What are the different activities we're performing that our competition is not?
2. What are the similar activities we're performing in a way that differs from our competition?

Operational Effectiveness

Perhaps the most common error is mistaking operational effectiveness for strategy. Operational effectiveness is the proverbial wolf in strategy's clothing. It means to perform similar activities in a similar manner as competitors, trying to do them a little better or faster. However, employing operational effectiveness without strategy is like running the same race as competitors, hoping only to be a little faster. Incorporating strategy indicates that we are going to run a course that differs from our competitors'—one that we ourselves have designed to win.

Look at nearly any industry and you'll see examples of established companies locked in battles of operational effectiveness. When companies become complacent and rely on doing the same things in the same ways as their competitors (e.g., United Airlines and American Airlines), differentiated entrants come into the marketplace and begin to take their business (e.g., Southwest Airlines). Author Michael Raynor provides additional support that differentiation is the path to profitability: "Drawing on a unique data set made available by Statistics Canada, it has been possible to replicate and validate on a much larger scale what earlier research had only suggested: that firms with clear product differentiation or cost leadership positions do in fact gain higher operating margins than firms that are 'stuck in the middle' between these two strategic positions."[10]

Outperform the Competition

The final component of the definition of business strategy is to outperform the competition in serving customers. Strategy inherently involves competition. The Latin origin of the word *competition* is *competere*, which means "to strive together."[11] The fact is, we've all been competing for a long time: think back to kickball at recess, the heart-pounding spelling bees, or Little League on Saturdays.

> Strategic leaders are continually asking: What are the different activities we're performing that our competition is not? and What are the similar activities we're performing in a way that differs from our competition?

When we were kids, we relied primarily on our physical attributes—such as size, speed, and strength—to win the day. As adults in business, we compete with attributes that reside in our minds. Today, it's the size, speed, and strength of our thinking that create and sustain competitive advantage. In fact, research out of Harvard University shows that competitive position accounts for 32 percent of the variation in profit across firms. This is nearly twice as important as the industry in which the firms compete.[12] It's in our relentless drive to raise our level of thinking—in our desire to compete, or "strive together"—that strategy becomes the glue that mentally binds us together to maximize our chances of succeeding in whatever market we play. In fact, there are three levels of competitive considerations that good leaders factor into their strategic thinking and planning to ensure a holistic approach: (1) industrial, (2) organizational, and (3) individual.

Industrial Level

The majority of your company's competitive efforts at the industrial level revolve around the other companies you compete with. This is also known as industry rivalry. Michael Porter, author of the landmark works *Competitive Strategy* and *Competitive Advantage*, points out, however, that "In essence, the job of the strategist is to understand and cope with competition. Often however, managers define competition too narrowly, as if it occurred only among today's direct competitors. Yet competition for profits goes beyond established industry rivals to include four other competitive forces as well: customers, suppliers, potential entrants, and substitute products."[13]

We compete with each of these forces for the profits of the industry. A thorough examination of each can provide insights as to which areas hold the most promise for enhancing your company's share of the profit pie. While we don't often think of customers as a competitive force, our interactions with them determine the respective slices of the profit pie. Suppliers are another competitive force to consider because the more money we pay to them for our cost of supplied goods and services, the less profit we keep. Potential entrants are an obvious threat, as the greater the number of players in our market, the more difficult it is to earn a healthy profit. The "substitutes" force can be particularly important: research by professors Mark Bergen and Margaret Peteraf has shown that among competitors with equivalent resources, indirect competitors pose the greatest threat to a focal company.[14] Unfortunately, if you were to conduct a competitive analysis of only the current industry competitors, you would entirely miss the indirect competitors, who can do the most damage to your business.

For example, if you own a flower shop, your direct competitors would include other local flower shops, landscaping centers, and online florists. However, there is a host of indirect competitors competing for the gift-giving aspect of flowers. The indirect competitors (substitutes) might include chocolate shops selling candy bouquets, stores selling greeting cards, grocery stores selling helium balloons, and bakeries selling cookie cakes (if nothing else, at least you now have some ideas for Valentine's Day!). As you think through your business at the industrial level, be sure to include all five factors, not just the direct industry rivals.

Organizational Level

A competitive consideration at the organizational level is the internal competition for resources among business units, functional groups, and company departments. These resources may include budget dollars, time on the agenda at the senior management meeting, and mindshare of the sales force. In midsize to large organizations, this can often be the most serious competitive threat. If senior management has not created a culture and compensation structure to encourage an equitable distribution of resources among internal groups, fiefdoms can develop. And once fiefdoms emerge, the internal battle for cash, talent, and time can often be bloodier than any of the external competitor battles.

Individual Level

The individual level of competitive consideration falls into two areas: you and your customers. One of the most dangerous aspects of competition resides in the minds of your customers. Changing customer behavior is often far more difficult than upending a competitor's offering.

As research on the human condition has shown time and again, when you introduce a new product or service, people are inherently predisposed to rejecting it because it will require risk and a change from the status quo. In fact, research has shown that 75 percent of new product launches fall significantly short of projections.[15]

Along with risk aversion and a preference for the status quo, apathy is another silent assassin. We tend to focus on giving prospective customers reams of data to change their product preference when it's often the emotional component that can win the day. For example, moving a customer from apathy to eager purchase is often not about statistics on the durability and longevity of an automobile tire versus other tires. It's about showing a picture of the customer's diaper-clad baby sitting in the tire to elicit the emotional element of the decision.

You must also compete with yourself, including your embedded biases, experiences, and frames of reference. A survey of 362 companies asked executives if they believed they delivered a "superior experience" to their customers, and 80 percent replied they did. When customers were asked about the level of performance in their experiences with the companies they bought from, merely 8 percent of those companies received a rating of "superior."[16] As the data show, our biases can dramatically alter our perception of reality.

You must also compete with your experience, as experience is often seen as an over-the-counter elixir for all that ails the business. There are countless examples of executives who fail to diagnose the changing context of their business and simply employ strategies and tactics that were successful in the past. If the current state of the business is different from the past, the chance of those same strategies and tactics continuing to be effective is dramatically reduced. Finally, competition comes in the frames you bring to your work, whether educational (engineers trained to think differently from marketers), functional (a sales executive focusing on different factors from a finance executive), or social (a type A individual acts differently from a type B individual). In order to defeat the tunnel vision that your own frames create, you must constantly challenge yourself with other perspectives from inside and outside the organization.

The ultimate test of any strategy is its ability to provide a superior level of value to customers. With a constant eye on the competition, it's easy to become obsessed with maneuvering on the competitive landscape. Unfortunately, that can eclipse the importance of what the customer values and undermine your best intentions. These usually take the form of "better" products featuring bells and whistles that customers really don't need or aren't willing to pay for. The intelligent allocation of limited resources must lead to superior value for the customer; otherwise, the only thing you'll be competing with is the red ink flowing from the business.

STRATEGY'S HOLY GRAIL—COMPETITIVE ADVANTAGE

For all the debate and consternation over what competitive advantage in business really is, one has only to look to nature and the good old wood frog for answers. The wood frog positions itself in the damp woodlands of various North American mountain ranges. When the brutal winter comes, it actually changes into another form of life, packing its cells with glucose (a natural antifreeze) and freezing its own fluid into crystals small enough not to damage itself. Fifteen hours after the first ice crystal forms, the wood frog is completely frozen, including its blood. It stays in suspended animation for the duration of the winter—with no heartbeat, no blood flow, and no breathing, which is normally the definition of death.

When spring arrives, the wood frog's heart is shocked back to life. Sparks from the static built up by the electrically charged chemicals are forced out by the stretching fibers of the heart muscle, reconnecting the wood frog to life. It is then free to enjoy the solitude offered by the competitive advantage of its domain. As this example demonstrates, achieving competitive advantage is really quite simple—as simple as being brought back from the dead. Fortunately in the business arena, understanding what constitutes competitive advantage and the methods of achieving it is not quite as drastic.

Professor Stephen Tallman of the University of Richmond offers us a reminder of why we embark on strategy in the first place. "Strategy has come to discuss the objective of competition as sustained competitive advantage. That is, the successful firm is one that demonstrates long-term advantage over its competition."[17]

Competitive advantage is defined as "an offering of superior value based on differences in capabilities and activities."

Competitive advantage comprises the following three components: capabilities, activities, and offerings (products and services). (See Figure 2.1 for a visual representation of these three components.)

Figure 2.1 Competitive Advantage

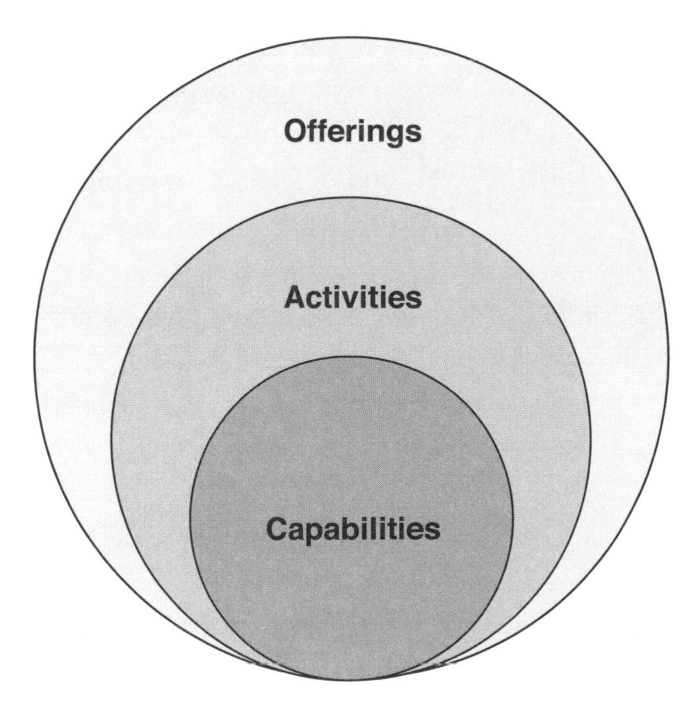

Capabilities

The genesis of products and services is capabilities, which are made up of resources and core competencies. Capabilities can be classified as one of two types: distinctive or reproducible. Distinctive capabilities are those that cannot be emulated by competitors or can only be emulated with extreme difficulty. Distinctive capabilities allow an organization to do things for less money than its rivals or to do something that its rivals simply cannot do. Reproducible capabilities are those that can be successfully replicated by competitors.

A fundamental component of sustainable competitive advantage is to have distinctive capabilities. These come in a variety of forms, including intellectual property, marketing expertise leading to strong brands, effective leadership, and organizational culture. Most initial searches for competitive advantage begin with the offerings themselves, examining products for such differentiating qualities as efficacy, safety, ease of use, convenience, etc. However, true competitive advantage takes root at the deeper level of capabilities. Additionally, research has shown that competitive advantage built on capabilities derived from resources is sustained by these four conditions:

1. Resources are heterogeneous, that is, different from firm to firm. If all firms have identical resources, it is difficult to gain an advantage.
2. Market for resources must not be equal in providing the same resources, or access to resources, across the board.
3. Market for products must vary in that resources are challenging to copy and difficult to replace with substitutes or alternatives.
4. Resources must not be mobile, or easily transferred from one firm to another, by being embedded in capabilities.[18]

Activities

Activities are where capabilities merge with resource allocation decisions to be transformed into the offerings that customers see. The activities selected to invest in—or not invest in—determine the strategic focus. The challenge most executives face trying to determine their competitive advantages is that they look at the entire organization or product as a whole. It's not until the organization or product is broken down into individual activities that a clearer assessment of competitive advantage emerges. Individual activities fall into categories, such as supply chain management, operations, marketing, distribution, and service relative to the offering. The combination of these activities is commonly referred to as the company's value chain. While these primary activities are what produce most of the value a customer sees (see Figure 2.2), they are supported by secondary activities, such as research and development, human resources, systems development, and other important tasks that facilitate the performance of the primary activities.

Figure 2.2 Value Chain

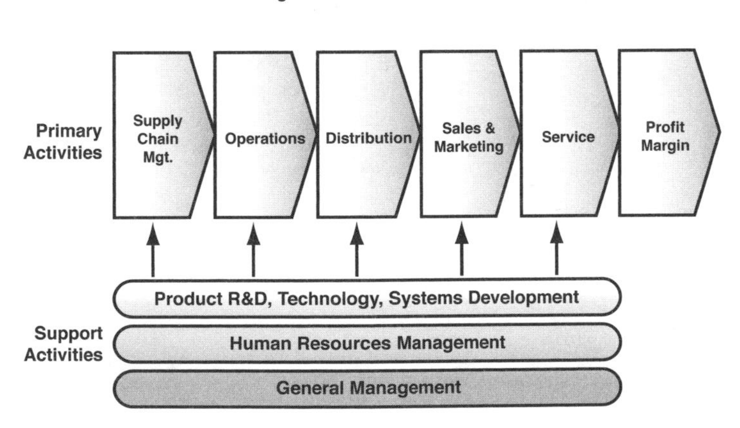

In performing this analysis of activities, it becomes clear that having multiple activities working in unison is a key driver of success. Relying solely on one differentiating activity to keep competitors at bay is like relying on one bullet to stop a charging rhinoceros. In either case, you're likely to get trampled.

Once the business is assessed at the individual activity level, the all-important relationships and linkages among activities can be evaluated. These linkages can lead to competitive advantage through both optimization (combining activities across functions to become more efficient or effective) and coordination (providing a seamless offering to customers).

Offerings

The weapons ultimately brandished in competitive battles come in the form of offerings. The offerings brought to the market embody the strategy and are the central element of competition among firms, providing the tangible representation of this competition to customers.

Competitive advantage comes through three steps:

1. Customers perceive a consistent difference among offerings, and that difference occurs in an attribute that affects the buying decision.
2. The difference in the offering stems from a distinctive capability.
3. Both the offering difference and the distinctive capability last over time.[19]

The process of assessing competitive advantage can be facilitated using a strategic thinking model to visualize the process. Recall the rental car example introduced earlier, and then refer to Figure 2.3 to make an objective analysis of competitive advantage between the market leaders Enterprise Rent-A-Car and Hertz.

Figure 2.3 Competitive Advantage Analysis

	Enterprise Rent-A-Car	Hertz
Capabilities	- Privately held - Recent college graduates - Small, inexpensive offices located in metro areas (6,900) - Older, soon-to-be-discontinued cars	- Publicly held - Expensive offices located at airports - New cars
Activities	- Deliver cars to customers' homes or rental sites or deliver customers to cars - In-house reservations - Grassroots marketing - Cultivate strong relationships with auto dealers, body shops. insurance adjusters - Enterprise Service Quality Index (prompt phone calls to 1 of every 15 customers)	- Customers pick up cars at airports - Outsource reservations - Advertising (TV) - Hertz Gold Program
Offerings	- Rental cars to temporarily replace cars being repaired or drivers needing an extra vehicle short-term at rates 1/3 less than main competitors'	- Rental cars for air travelers

In examining the chart, it's apparent that Enterprise Rent-A-Car's differing capabilities (privately held; staffed by recent college graduates; located in small inexpensive offices in metro areas; and older, soon-to-be-discontinued cars) fuel the activities that provide its target market with a distinct offering (home/city replacement cars) that provides superior value (cars delivered to customers at a rate that is 30 percent less than airport rentals) to its targeted customers.

If, after going through this process, your organization determines that it is at a competitive disadvantage, you can choose among several options to transform that disadvantage into an advantage.

1. Change the offerings, creating better alignment between the capabilities and the offerings (e.g., Whirlpool's innovative appliances).

2. Create new capabilities (e.g., Apple's move into digital music).
3. Influence customer preference by changing the relevance criteria or making the value of the offering clearer (e.g., Subway's emphasis on healthy fast food).
4. Change the game—innovate into the market white space, where competition is nonexistent (e.g., Cirque du Soleil).[20]

What's frustrating for managers who are trying to achieve competitive advantage is that it is seldom a quick process. True competitive advantage begins with making fundamental resource allocation decisions regarding capabilities. In many companies, shifting or focusing resources, especially head count, to create or develop capabilities that may not immediately translate into short-term results can be a Herculean task. Consequently, few companies dedicate themselves to achieving true competitive advantage. So, the next time you're debating whether to risk making a sizable resource allocation to create distinct capabilities, remember the wood frog. After all, it's not as difficult as coming back from the dead.

VALUE DISCIPLINE SPELLS SUCCESS

Complementing the work of understanding strategy and beginning to clear a path for competitive advantage is the concept of value disciplines. Research by Michael Treacy and Fred Wiersema conducted among more than eighty market-leading companies demonstrated that successful organizations can be categorized by one of three distinct value disciplines: product leadership, operational excellence, and customer intimacy.[21]

Successful companies, research shows, choose one of the three value disciplines to excel in and maintain industry-average thresholds in the other two (see Figure 2.4). From a strategy perspective, that means the majority of a firm's discretionary resources are allocated toward only one of the three areas. This principle flies in the face of the human tendency toward balance and equilibrium; yet, great strategy requires trade-offs in order to load resources into one area and put only a threshold amount in the other two value disciplines.

> By focusing on one of the value disciplines—product leadership, operational excellence, or customer intimacy—you will create momentum for your business that competitors simply cannot match.

Figure 2.4 Value Disciplines

Product Leadership

As one would guess, product leadership is all about providing the best product, one that offers true differentiated value in the marketplace. Successful product leaders produce products and services that customers recognize as the best, offerings that add significant benefits and performance to them. The product leaders' primary source of competition is themselves: they work fast and furiously to make their older offerings obsolete by introducing their own new state-of-the-art products. Examples of product leadership companies include Nike, 3M, and Apple. They understand that they provide premium brands, and more importantly, they build value propositions that enable them to command premium prices for their brands. From a strategy perspective, the majority of their resources are allocated to their people and R&D efforts—the two primary sources of continued product superiority and innovation.

Operational Excellence

Companies that focus on the operational excellence value discipline are characterized as having the best total cost. They provide customers with reliable offerings at competitive prices and deliver those offerings in an efficient manner. Examples include Wal-Mart, Southwest Airlines, McDonald's, and FedEx. These companies realize that standardization and efficiency are the lifeblood of their businesses.

Customer Intimacy

Customer-intimate firms offer the best total solution. They live on the depth and length of relationships with their customers—relationships built on understanding exactly what customers need and how to deliver it in a tailored fashion. Companies that focus on this value discipline include IBM, GE, and Nordstrom.

Not having the discipline or the understanding to select and emphasize a single value discipline results in three undesirable

DIVE MASTER PRACTICE

In the next management meeting, explain the concept of the three value disciplines along with examples and ask each person to write on a note card which of the three disciplines your group is using to drive the business. Having facilitated this exercise with organizations all over the world, I can tell you that it's rare for everyone to list the same one. If your managers have different views on what's driving the success of the business, it's a good bet their strategic initiatives are not aligned either. The value disciplines can be an effective compass for agreeing on direction and focus.

effects: (1) fractured strategic direction, (2) weakened brand, and (3) mediocrity and commoditization. These negative effects quietly suffocate a business because they prevent people from harnessing the power that comes from the intense focus of time, talent, and money. By focusing on one of the value disciplines—and thereby avoiding these negative effects—you will create momentum for your business that competitors simply cannot match.

Fractured Strategic Direction

A fractured strategic direction occurs when an organization lacks the discipline to focus the majority of its resources on just one of the three areas of value. Usually, in a well-meaning but ill-conceived attempt to grow the business, their resources begin migrating to several of the value disciplines. This resource migration muddies the strategic direction and compromises growth in the long term. Truly successful companies are committed to excelling in only one of the three disciplines while maintaining parity in the other two.

Weakened Brand

Aligning a group around a focus on one of the three value disciplines is a critical component of robust strategy. One of the primary challenges is ensuring that all of the different functional areas are "singing from the same song sheet." It's quite common for the marketing and R&D teams to be working and promoting from the product leadership value discipline while the sales force is selling on low price. This internal conflict blurs the value of the offering to customers and creates false expectations, and the end result is a weakened brand in the marketplace.

Mediocrity and Commoditization

Allocating resources evenly among the three value disciplines is the most insidious cause of business failure. This even distribution prevents a company from realizing its true potential and condemns it to the slow and steady damnation of surviving instead of thriving. When individuals in an organization are not galvanized around one of the three value disciplines, the result is a watered-down, mediocre offering that lacks valuable differentiation, which can come only from extreme focus.

PEARLS OF INSIGHT

- **Strategy is not:**
    1. Aspiration: goals, objectives, or visions
    2. Best practices: trying to be better than instead of different from the competition
    3. Caution: being tentative and restrained, afraid to make trade-offs
- ***Business strategy* is defined as "the intelligent allocation of limited resources through a unique system of activities to outperform the competition in serving customers."**
- **Principle of Competitive Exclusion: "No two members of the same species can coexist that make their livings in the identical way."**
- **There are two lenses of strategy:**
    1. Performing different activities from the competition
    2. Performing similar activities in a different way from the competition
- **There are three levels of competition:**
    1. Industrial
    2. Organizational
    3. Individual

- **_Competitive advantage_ is defined as "an offering of superior value based on differences in capabilities and activities."**
- **There are three Value Disciplines:**
    1. Product Leadership—best total product
    2. Operational Excellence—best total cost
    3. Customer Intimacy—best total solution

CHAPTER 3

DISCIPLINE #1: ACUMEN—THE DEEP DIVE FOR INSIGHT

Dive into the sea of thought, and find there pearls beyond price.

—Moses Ibn Ezra, philosopher and poet

One of the interesting paradoxes of strategy is that in order to elevate your thinking to see "the big picture," you must first dive below the surface of the issues to uncover insight. A strategic insight is a new idea that combines two or more pieces of information to affect the overall success of the business and lead to competitive advantage. An image of an iceberg will help to illustrate how companies use insight. Universally, organizations battle one another using only obvious information, which can be represented by the tip of the iceberg. The tip, however, does not reveal the precious insights hidden below the surface of the business. Relying on the information above the surface of the water—in plain sight and readily available to all—requires no extra effort. It is the path of least resistance and is chosen by those too lazy to do any real thinking (i.e., Beach Bums and Snorkelers). Since the information is readily available to the entire market, it quickly loses value when you are trying to develop a strategy that relies on differentiation to gain competitive advantage.

To gain true strategic insight, you must dive deep below the surface—like a Scuba Diver or a Free Diver does—to explore the largest portion of the iceberg. In Figure 3.1, the large size of the underwater portion of the iceberg indicates the larger impact unleashing these insights will have on a business. If you've ever experienced a period of static sales or price wars, it's reasonable to assume you were competing with tip-of-the-iceberg information. In difficult economic times, the organizations whose managers are able to generate subsurface insights are able to break away from the pack and carve out profitable growth.

One example of this principle can be found in the software industry. Founded in 1995, Red Hat provides companies with operating system platforms, middleware, applications, and consulting

Figure 3.1 Insight Iceberg

services. Red Hat has become known as a dominant distributor of Linux open-source software. It was subsurface insight that led to its leadership position in the market.

As the market continued to evolve, software companies chose to build their offerings on one of two primary business models. One model was to provide open-source software with a low product price, and the other was to provide proprietary software driven by profitable service. These models represented the tip of the iceberg—open-source software with a low price or proprietary software with a high price.

Bob Young, a cofounder of Red Hat, discovered a base-of-the-iceberg, or subsurface insight: combine the open-source software model's low price with the proprietary model's service offering.[1] This spawned a new software category called Software as a Service, or SaaS, as it's referred to in the industry. This insight ignited Red Hat's growth and led to the creation of a corporate market for the Linux operating system. In December 2005, *CIO Insight* magazine published the results of its Vendor Value Survey and Red Hat ranked #1 for the second year in a row. The Red Hat example illustrates a key tenet: insight is the product of two or more bits of information that are combined in a unique way.[2]

INSIGHT—STRATEGY'S STARTING POINT

Strategists need to build their thinking around insights and how to discover them. If a company can come up with true insights, then developing a strategy to exploit them is a viable task. Developing a strategy without insights is dangerous because it leads to unrealistic plans.

—Andrew Campbell, former professor, Harvard Business School

The challenge of generating insight is not confined to the world of business. The ability to generate insight is important in any area where new thinking is required to create new value or, in some cases, to prevent loss. The inability to generate insights can have devastating effects, as the events of September 11, 2001, remind us. Authors Tim Laseter and Rob Cross point out, "As the investigations after September 11, 2001, have shown, the greatest challenge in the world of intelligence gathering occurs not in data collection, but in making the connections that generate insight."[3]

Most organizations are swimming in more information than they know what to do with. The true challenge is to piece together the salient points and gain insight. Too often in organizations the lack of insight is shielded by a wall of data that appears to be useful but offers little in the way of practical application or progress. Robert Brullo, a former executive at 3M, which in the past was known for its insight prowess, says: "To me, the point is to communicate an insight, not simply a bunch of numbers or a bunch of bullet points. It keeps coming down to the same thing—you have to be able to show that the insight is there."[4]

The fact that so many organizations continue to cling to the absurd practice of asking their managers to build ninety-five-slide PowerPoint decks through which to present their annual strategic plans screams, "We have no insight!" If managers are not able to clearly and concisely present in one or two slides what their business is, it's for one reason: they don't know the business. And when you don't know the business, insights aren't going to pop out and introduce themselves. James Hackett, CEO of Steelcase, shares his experience with this issue: "In our initial product development meetings, marketing folks would present PowerPoint slides of product ideas and I would say, 'What's the user insight that led to this product?' They would give me this look like I [had] asked an unfair question."[5]

Organizations do their managers no favors by perpetuating this issue. The data reveal that 85 percent of executive management teams spend less than one hour a month discussing strategy, with 50 percent spending no time at all.[6] It's no wonder many managers actually feel guilty taking time to think strategically. In our action-dominated society, where the motto "greed is good" has been replaced by "speed is good," it seems managers are uncomfortable investing time to think for fear they'll be associated with Auguste Rodin's statue *The Thinker*—an immovable, noncontributing, huddled figure with chin on hand and bird droppings on head.

The accomplishments of Nobel Prize–winning physicist Luis Alvarez are prime examples of the importance of taking time to think and generate insights. His "thinking" accomplishments include among others: the theory that asteroids hitting the Earth caused the extinction of dinosaurs; the invention of an aircraft blind-landing system called the Ground Controlled Approach system; and the discovery of a large number of resonance states, made possible through his development of the technique of using a hydrogen bubble chamber and data analysis for which he won the Nobel Prize. Dr. Alvarez credits his father with giving him the advice that shaped his career. Walter Alvarez, a renowned physician and prolific writer of medical textbooks, counseled Luis to invest time each day to ponder his work and his studies. Luis took this advice to heart and spent a half hour each day to think about what he had learned and to record his observations.[7]

Joel Klein, chancellor for the New York City public schools, also understands the value of taking time to think strategically. Despite overseeing 1.1 million students and 80,000 teachers, Klein doesn't allow his schedule to be swallowed up by activity for activity's sake. He says: "I learned when I was in the federal government that most people like to go to meetings all day and I just don't. I try to block out chunks of time where I can read things more easily and think through the next moves and strategies. I'll have an hour of just think time. I make that part of my schedule."[8]

Just as it's important for individuals to take time to think strategically, research shows that it's critical for teams to do so as well. Studies by Mark Jung-Beeman of Northwestern University's Institute for Neuroscience have shown that in order for insights to be useful, they need to be generated from within, as opposed to being handed to people in a written report.[9] The adrenaline rush that occurs when an insight is generated occurs only when a person goes through the experience of connecting two or more pieces of information him- or herself. (Consider the Beach Bum or Snorkeler's limited knowledge of an iceberg compared to that of the Scuba and Free divers.) The moment of insight is also known to create a positive, euphoric state which is integral to driving the change in mind-set necessary to implement the insight.[10] Consequently, scheduling regular forums for group strategic thinking not only is a valuable method of generating insights but also provides an excellent means of building strategic thinking skill sets within all members of a team.

The adrenaline rush that occurs when an insight is generated happens only when a person goes through the experience of connecting two or more pieces of information him- or herself.

SOURCES OF INSIGHT

It is assumed in some circles that acumen is a static state that someone either possesses or doesn't. However, when the sources for producing insight are brought to light, it is quickly evident that given the proper instruction and tools managers can be taught to think strategically on a regular basis. Beach Bums and Snorkelers can use four primary sources of insight to transform themselves into Scuba

Divers and Free Divers: (1) context, (2) customers, (3) questions, and (4) models.

Context

The central lesson we can take from business history
is that context matters. The ability to understand the zeitgeist
and pursue the unique opportunities it presents
for each company is what separates the truly great
from the merely competent.

—Nitin Nohria, professor, Harvard Business School

On a cold, gray February morning, an airline captain wakes up at 4:00 o'clock and drives from his home in the northern suburbs of Chicago to O'Hare Airport to pilot a 6:30 a.m. flight to New York's JFK Airport. When he arrives he's handed the weather report, which notes the wind direction, wind speed, temperature, precipitation, cloud ceiling, etc. He tosses the report into the nearest garbage can without even glancing at it. He enters the cockpit and immediately starts the engines without going through any of the nearly seventy items of the preflight checklist.

An hour into the flight, the plane makes a crash landing near Toledo, Ohio. A number of passengers are injured. Later that afternoon, investigators ask the pilot about his total disregard for the preflight procedures, which are designed to help pilots fully understand the situation they are departing from in order to increase the probability of a successful flight. The pilot replies: "Look, I'm much too busy flying as fast as I can from city to city to be slowed down by some preflight checklist. That may be fine for some pilots, but I'm a 'fly first and ask questions later' type of guy."

If you recall hearing about this near-tragic accident a few years ago, please grab another cup of coffee, because it's fictional. Nevertheless, although the details are fictitious, the issue of not having the time or using the tools to understand the context, or current situation, is all too real in the business world. Failing to think through the business context may not have the frightening effect of a plane crash, but it can result in losing your job, income, retirement savings, or funds for children's education and in organizational bankruptcy. Ask Kevin Rollins, former CEO of Dell, who said the following shortly before he was fired: "The competitive environment has been more intense than we had planned for or understood."[11] Or go back to one of the most influential business leaders in history, Alfred P. Sloan, CEO of General Motors in the 1920s and '30s. Despite the fact that his ideas shaped the structure of the modern corporation, he was relieved of his duties because he failed to understand and acknowledge the emerging role of the United Automobile Workers union.[12]

The importance of context is evident in all walks of life including dining, entertainment, and sports. Le Français, a Chicago-area restaurant once rated the best in America by *Bon Appétit* magazine, closed its doors in 2007 after thirty-four years in business. *Chicago Tribune* food critic Phil Vettel wrote: "The food, under Chef Roland Liccioni, was as good as ever. The servers, some who had been with the restaurant for twenty years or more, remained their charming and disarming selves. What had changed was the competition."[13] Failure to understand and adapt to the changing context can ruin even the most successful of companies. As Charles Darwin said, "It's not the strongest of the species who survive, nor even the most intelligent, but the ones most responsive to change."

Katie Couric, former NBC *Today* show star, was paid $15 million a year to become anchor of the *CBS Evening News*. After six months, her telecast was in last place behind *ABC World News* (9.6 million viewers) and *NBC Nightly News* (9.4 million viewers), with only 7.5 million viewers. Her numbers were even down 400,000 viewers from the same time the previous year when interim anchor Bob Schieffer was in the chair.[14]

How context can determine a person's success or failure can be seen as well in coaches who move from the collegiate level to the professional level. The following basketball coaches were extremely successful at the college level and then failed miserably at the professional level, as evidenced by their winning percentages (college versus pro):

- Rick Pitino (.814/ .411)
- John Calipari (.731/ .391)
- Tim Floyd (.633/ .220)
- Jerry Tarkanian (.829/ .450)

What contributed to Le Français's, Couric's, and the coaches' failures? Their context changed, and a different context often requires different skills. Former Harvard Business School professor Theodore Levitt provides the reminder, "For all the talk about management as a science, experienced executives know that strategic decisions and tactics depend heavily on context."[15]

Unwrapping Context

Context is defined by the *American Heritage Dictionary* as "the circumstances in which an event occurs; a setting."[16] To refer once more to GE's CEO, in his 2003 letter to shareholders, Jeff Immelt wrote: "Two important lessons were reinforced for me last year: the value of context and the importance of driving change. By 'context' I mean understanding important trends and their impact on GE."[17] Research by Yankelovich Partners showed that half of the executives surveyed rated their organizations below average in their ability to identify critical issues within their business.[18]

The inability to understand context is at the heart of numerous failures. There are three pitfalls of context to avoid if you are to be successful: (1) annual assessment, (2) relative versus absolute performance, and (3) prescription without diagnosis.

Annual Assessment From a business-planning perspective, context is often expressed as the "situational analysis." The problem with this is that business planning generally happens once a year in most organizations, if that (nearly 40 percent of organizations have no formal business-planning process).[19] This means that the majority of managers don't have a solid understanding of the context of their business. This is like attempting to map out driving directions to a destination without knowing whence the car is leaving. It's the "You Are Here" map at the museum minus the big red dot to indicate where you are. Niccolo Machiavelli wrote the following in *The Prince*: "I have often reflected that the causes of the successes or failures of men are dependent on their ability to suit their manner to the times."[20] And, as they say, "The times, they are a-changing"—usually more than once a year.

Relative versus Absolute Performance The second pitfall of context is the failure to understand that performance is relative, not absolute. This means that an organization's improvement in operations or customer service or new product offerings may mean nothing at all to the market if the competition has improved or differentiated itself at a higher rate. Organizations that continue to wear the inward blinders and not pay attention to changes in the market dynamics and competitive landscape are at the greatest risk. Quoting Mintzberg once again, "As position, strategy encourages us to look at organizations in context, specifically in their competitive environments—how they decide on their products and markets and protect them in order to meet competition, avoid it or subvert it."[21]

If strategy's goal is to achieve competitive advantage, then awareness of the environment must be kept in mind when considering and designing that competitive advantage. Again, getting better at what you do is nice, but it means little if it's not also recognized by customers as superior to the competition. Oxford University lecturer Robert Pitkethly sounds a final foghorn: "Competitive advantage is in fact meaningless as a concept unless it is used in the context of a given competitive environment. An advantage has to be gained over something other than the possessor of the advantage, in respect of some criteria relevant to a common objective and in relation to a given location and competitive environment. Competitive advantage depends on context."[22]

> Getting better at what you do is nice, but it means little if it's not also recognized by customers as superior to the competition.

Prescription without Diagnosis Remember the visit to the doctor's office described during the discussion of the Strategic Thinking Assessment in chapter 1? Again, imagine you're sitting in your physician's office and she walks in, takes one look at you, scribbles out a prescription, and says, "Take one of these a day and call me in a week." You reply, "But you didn't even ask me what's wrong." She responds, "I gave these to my last three patients and they all got better, so I know they'll work for you."

This is ridiculous, not only in a medical situation; it also is not appropriate for any business situation, though it happens all the time. A company's sales are declining and someone picks up one of the many "prescription books." The book says that if you do what successful companies have done (e.g., "break all the rules," "create a customer-centric organization," "innovate or die," etc.), your firm will also rocket to stardom. What the majority of these books don't do is clearly diagnose the context that the organizations were in as they ascended their stairways to success. Without a keen understanding of their contexts or yours, it's impossible to determine if the business prescription will indeed "cure what ails you." Harvard Business School professor Clayton Christensen puts it this way: "It is the ability to begin thinking and acting in a circumstance-contingent way that brings predictability to strategy and innovation.

Rather than using one-size-fits-all strategies and methods in managing innovation, managers who are armed with sound, circumstance-contingent theories can artfully take the approach in each different situation that will be effective in that circumstance."[23]

A study of electronic warfare technicians who varied in experience level from six months to seven years was conducted to assess their decision-making abilities. The authors concluded with this statement: "The results showed that the experts placed a greater emphasis on the situation analysis (context) while the majority of novices emphasized deciding on the course of action."[24] When it comes to thoughtful action, the same principle as the old carpenter's adage applies: assess context twice and act once.

Navigating the Fog of Context

Each day we're consumed by whirlpools of activity that mentally hurl us around like socks in a washing machine. When we resurface after a half-day of back-to-back-to-back meetings, only to be greeted by forty-five new e-mails and nine voice messages, it's easy to see how we can quickly lose track of our business. There are three tools we can use to keep our heads above water and effectively gauge the context of the business: (1) strategy tune-up sessions, (2) OODA Loop, and (3) contextual radar.

Strategy Tune-up Sessions Those who drive a car every day wouldn't dream of going an entire year without a tune-up to check fluid levels, gauge tire pressure, change the oil, replace filters, etc. Nevertheless, while we regularly check our $35,000 automobiles, we wait a full year (and sometimes longer) to do a diagnostic check on our multimillion- or multibillion-dollar businesses. Now *that* makes sense!

A simple solution is to conduct periodic (weekly, monthly, or quarterly) strategy tune-ups to check on the context of the business.

The focus of these sessions isn't to arrive at new conclusions; rather, it's to openly discuss the four areas that constitute the context of the business: market, customers, competitors, and the company. The goal is to find changes in the context of the business and use the resulting insights to leverage opportunities and to blunt threats in a timely manner. Honda has used this technique (called "Nimawashi sessions" in Japan) with great success as one of the pillars of its strategic action plans.

OODA Loop A second tool that can be used to navigate context is the OODA Loop, developed by former U.S. Air force fighter pilot Colonel John Boyd.[25] The OODA (which stands for Observation, Orientation, Decision, Action) Loop (see Figure 3.2) is a mental framework that one can cycle through regularly to rapidly decode the environment, allocate resources, and act decisively.

Figure 3.2 OODA Loop

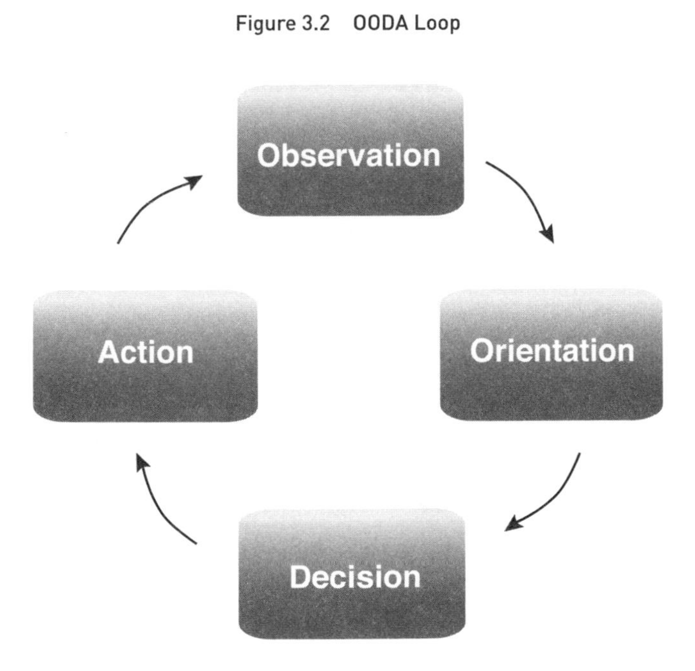

The OODA Loop acts as a reminder to continually observe (collect data and facts from the environment), orient (analyze and synthesize the data to form an educated perspective), decide (set a course through resource allocation), and act (execute the decisions). Used regularly, the OODA Loop can help your business adapt to changing circumstances through the heightened awareness and subsequent perspective of the situation.

Contextual Radar The final tool for consideration is the contextual radar. Radar is a method of detecting objects and determining their positions, velocities, or other characteristics using high-frequency radio waves reflected from their surfaces. In a similar fashion, the contextual radar provides a visual snapshot of the business situation. As seen in Figure 3.3, the four primary components of business—market, customers, competitors, and the company—each occupy a quarter of the radar screen. Surrounding the perimeter are the *what, who, where,* and *when* that need to be addressed for each

Figure 3.3 Contextual Radar

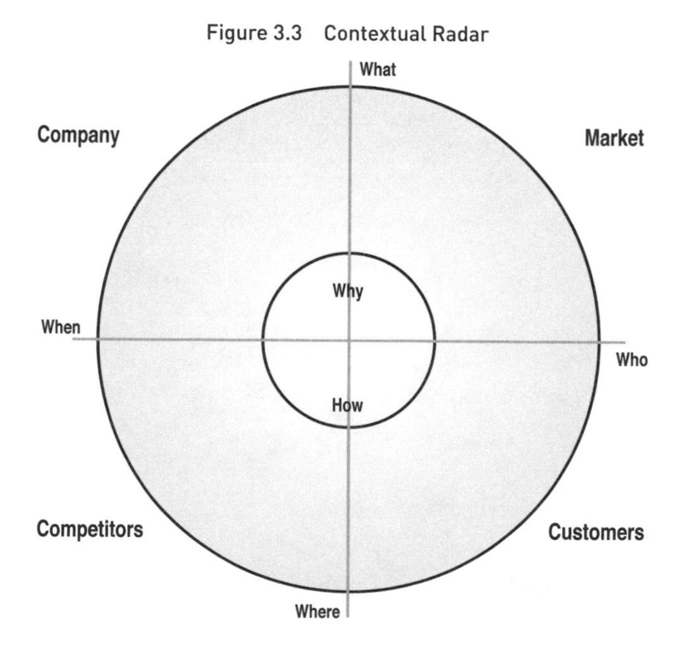

area. At the center of the radar are the reasons *why* these things are happening and *how* they have occurred.

Figure 3.4 further shows the highlights of an internal and external environmental scan using the contextual radar grid. This simple graphic provides a brief snapshot of the key components of a firm's context and makes it easy to communicate these insights to other members of a team, a business unit, or the organization as a whole.

This passage from the *Oxford Handbook of Strategy* reinforces the importance of having a radar-type mechanism in a business: "It is just as important to . . . recognize the changes sooner than competitors and to then . . . exploit that understanding. This stresses the importance of the company's business radar or means of gathering relevant and timely information but also the company's ability to process that information quickly and efficiently in order to include it in the strategic thinking of the company."[26]

Pilots run through preflight checklists, physicians conduct a battery of diagnostic tests, and managers check their BlackBerrys every

Figure 3.4 Contextual Radar Example

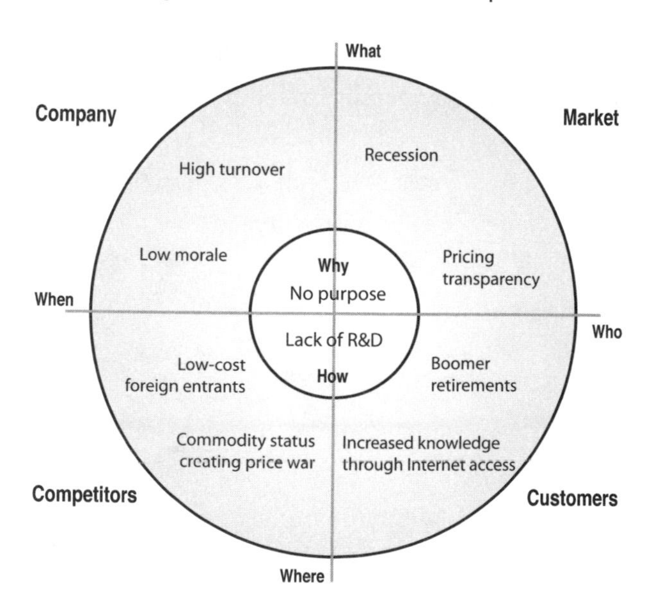

five minutes. To modify a popular adage, if you don't know where you're going, there's a good chance you have no idea where you are in the first place. Successfully navigating context means being able to choose the right action in the right place at the right time. And remember, understanding context is the first source of insight.

Customers

Although customers can be a rich source of insight into one's offerings, history suggests that customers themselves do not actually request many innovations. The error many organizations make is to use customers to help them determine future offerings. A partial list of the products that were not spawned from market research, or actually were predicted to fail according to market research with customers, includes the lightbulb, copy machines, minivans, Walkman portable music devices, personal computers, and Post-It notes, to name but a few. Author Kevin Coyne explains how customers play a minor role in product innovation: "Customers can tell you if they perceive your product to be inferior to competitor's offerings in some particular way. However, they can rarely tell you whether they need or want a product they have never seen or imagined. Market research can be invaluable in getting reactions to an idea once it is fully formed and tangibly demonstrated to the customer. It rarely, however, finds the latent need."[27]

Bob Lutz, GM's former vice chairman, echoes those sentiments: "The customer is at best just a rear-view mirror. He can tell you what he likes among the choices already out there. But when it comes to the future, why expect the customer to be the expert in clairvoyance or in creativity? After all, isn't that really what he expects us to be?"[28]

Numerous organizations employ some rendition of a "Voice of the Customer" program to establish an ongoing dialogue with their customers. These programs are an important way to gauge customer satisfaction with current offerings and service levels, and they are helpful in building relationships. However, solely listening to customers will generally not unearth the deeper needs they have. Companies such as Procter & Gamble have embraced the art of observation. Jim Stengel, chief marketing officer of P&G, says: "One key way the company now generates learning and intelligence is by encouraging its people to spend more time in the field with customers. The obvious needs of consumers typically have already been met and the real challenge lies in defining unarticulated needs."[29]

A new business focus has sprouted up in the area of ethnography, which is the branch of anthropology that deals with the study of specific human cultures and behaviors. The investment in ethnography is built on the premise that while customers aren't able to articulate their latent needs, their behaviors often provide the key insights that uncover them. James Dyson, whose innovative line of vacuum cleaners has stampeded the U.S. market and helped build a billion-dollar company, says: "I like frustration. I like seeing things in everyday life that don't work very well and try to make them better."[30]

In addition to observing customers, we can put ourselves in their shoes, or in one case, their cars. Toyota has risen to a leadership position in the U.S. automobile market by applying the Japanese philosophy of *genchi genbutsu*, which means "go and see." Toyota's chief engineer for the 2004 Sierra Minivan practiced the go-and-see philosophy by driving in all fifty states, as well as in Canada and Mexico, to generate insights. His driving experience inspired a redesign of the minivan to create a larger interior, greater turning radius, and side-wind stability.[31]

Customers can play a major role in the development and refinement of your company's offerings. As these examples have demonstrated, the adage "actions speak louder than words" was never truer than in the area of generating insights from customers. It may be tempting to turn over the decision-making process for offerings to the judgment of customers because they are, after all, the customer. But a final word of caution is in order, and it comes from Harvard

Business School professor Joseph Bower, who authored the 1970 landmark work *Managing the Resource Allocation Process*: "Our conclusion is that a primary reason why such firms lose their positions of industry leadership when faced with certain types of technological change has little to do with technology itself . . . Rather, they fail because they listen too carefully to their customers—and customers place stringent limits on the strategies firms can and cannot pursue."[32]

Questions

A third source of insights comes from questions. Questions stimulate thinking in new ways by posing a mental speed bump that makes us stop and evaluate. As children, we were taught to focus on answers, not questions, and this trend continues through adulthood. Answers give us confidence and closure; questions leave us anxious and unsure. It's no wonder that those individuals who consistently pose questions are seen, in many cases, as a hindrance to progress because they're always slowing things down. Asking the right question at the right time, however, can be a valuable gift to moving thinking forward. Jamie Dimon, CEO of JPMorgan Chase, says: "If you run a business—I think it's true on almost any level—once a month you sit down and go through it. What are the facts? What are the numbers? What did you say? What happened? What can you learn? What is the competition doing? What's working? What's not working?"[33]

Creative Insight–Generation Process

Questions also fuel the creative process for generating insights that psychologist Mihaly Csikszentmihalyi and advertising agency executive James Young have each identified independently in their books. I have gleaned five steps from their writings for what I call the creative insight–generation process that can jump-start your own insight efforts.[34, 35]

1. Prepare your mind by gathering information relative to the issue. The first step is the analysis portion, where the issue is broken down into its individual parts. Record these individual pieces of information in a journal or write the key facts separately on 3 x 5 note cards.
2. Think about the issue. Study the information, constantly rearranging it and looking for new relationships or associations. This is the synthesis portion of the process where we are looking to create new insights, or a new whole, from the reconfigured pieces of information.
3. Let the problem incubate in your subconscious and don't actively think about it. Occupy your time with other activities, from a walk by the lake, to attending a concert, to a day of playing in the park with the kids. The key is to free the conscious mind from actively thinking about the issue. A study by psychologist Ap Dijksterhuis of the University of Amsterdam validates this important step in the process. Professor Dijksterhuis showed participants complex information about potential apartments, roommates, and decorations. The first group was asked to state their immediate preference after reviewing a dozen pieces of information about four apartments. The second group was given a few minutes to consciously assess the information, and they made slightly better decisions than the first group. A third group proved, study after study, to make the best decisions, however, because their attention was distracted for a time. This enabled their minds to process the complex information unconsciously and make better decisions with superior results.[36]
4. The "Eureka!" moment will occur, where the new insight suddenly emerges. It is common for the eureka moment to occur in non-work-related activities, such as a morning shower or reading a favorite novel.

5. Evaluate the insight and apply it to the issue. After the initial excitement of identifying the potential insight, the less-exciting aspect of transforming the insight into tangible business value takes place. When Thomas Edison said that creativity is 1 percent inspiration and 99 percent perspiration, he was acknowledging the challenge of this final step.

Too often, we rely on haphazard group brainstorming sessions to generate new ideas. The creative-insight generation process gives us a proven way to stir up our thinking. It provides a means of nurturing our individual creative juices and opens our eyes to our true potential.

SCAMPER Technique

Questions are also at the heart of the SCAMPER technique created by Michael Michalko. This uses an array of thought-provoking questions around seven areas to initiate new ways of strategically thinking.[37] Changing your perspective often opens up uncharted areas of discovery to you that can lead to innovation. SCAMPER stands for Substitute, Combine, Adapt, Magnify/Modify, Put (to other uses), Eliminate, and Reverse/Rearrange. For each of the areas, sample questions are provided to catalyze thinking.

Substitute

- What product features could I substitute?
- Are there other external resources that can replace what I'm using?
- Is there something more cost-effective or environmentally friendly I could use in place of what I'm currently using?
- Is there another source for the raw materials?

Combine

- What product can I use in combination with it?
- Can I combine this product with a complementary service offering?
- Are there any unusual combinations I haven't thought of?
- Which successful service ideas from other industries can I combine with my offering?

Adapt

- How can this service evolve into something new?
- What changes could be made to update this product?
- Are there any products in other industries that perform a similar function that I could model this after?
- How have past successful products in this industry adapted to maintain market leadership?

Magnify/Modify

- Which product attributes can be magnified through promotion to increase sales?
- What opportunities can be magnified to capture greater market share?
- How can the service be modified to satisfy additional customer needs?
- Can we modify the sales channel to reach more of the target market?
- What features can be changed to make the service appealing to other demographic market segments?

Put (to other uses)

- How else can this product be used?

- Have customers used this product in any innovative ways?
- Are there product line extensions that make sense?
- Where can I reallocate my resources to become more successful?
- Which strategic initiatives have underperformed, and where can I reallocate their resources for greater success?

Eliminate

- What part of the customer purchasing process can I eliminate to make it faster and easier for customers to buy?
- Which reports or paperwork can I eliminate to give the sales force more time to be in the field selling?
- What steps in the service process are not adding value and can be eliminated?
- Which customers are not profitable to service and can be let go through attrition?

Reverse/Rearrange

- How can I rearrange the sales and marketing functions to be more customer friendly?
- What could we do to reverse the sales process—having our customers come to us instead of having our employees go to them?
- Could we use interactive technology to have our customers rearrange the product offering to tailor it to their individual needs?
- How would reversing the product development process affect the output?

The next time your business is stuck in a rut and there doesn't seem to be anything new you can do, pull out the SCAMPER technique and watch the ideas fly. While we're all looking for answers, this exercise shows that true value is oftentimes in the questions we ask.

Innovation Box

The Innovation Box is designed to generate new combinations from existing factors that will yield breakthrough ideas. First developed by Dr. Fritz Zwicky and called the Morphological Box, the Innovation Box is a tool that forces you to look at a wide variety of potential applications.[38] It is constructed by creating a box with seven columns and seven rows and then listing each of seven characteristics of the product/service individually as the heading of a column. The answers to the question, What are the variations of each characteristic? are then each listed below their respective characteristics, filling the six remaining cells of the column. When the cells of the Innovation Box have been filled, circle one variation of each characteristic and consider the new combination of factors that has been created. Continue using different variations of characteristics until you have generated enough new combinations to create an innovative approach to the challenge.

An Innovation Box represents almost a million possible combinations. The potential combinations change or morph as seemingly unrelated values are listed under each column and two or more columns are combined. Figure 3.5 is an example of the Innovation Box being created by a writing instrument company. The Innovation Box takes the complex process of innovatively conquering a challenge and provides an easy-to-use template that's sure to generate some new ideas.

Using questioning techniques such as the Creative Insight-Generation Process, SCAMPER, and the Innovation Box can fan the flames of insight discovery. As renowned strategist Keniche Ohmae reminds us, "The strategist's method is to challenge the prevailing assumptions with a single question: Why?"[39]

Figure 3.5 Innovation Box for Writing Instrument Company

Shape	Material	Texture	Size	Add-ons	Flexibility	Life
Round	Beaded	Soft	Person	Light	360	10,000 word
Square	Plastic	Hard	Finger	Scanner	Rigid	Lifetime
Hexagon	Wood	Spongy	Fingernail	Clips	Inflates	Disposable
Custom	Metal	Rubbery	Toothpick	Lighter	Shrinks	Refillable
Changes	Paper	Smooth	Straw	Eraser	Memory	Water base
Sculpted	Glass	Pebbled	Hand	White-out	Non-crush	Custom
Globe	Leaves	Edible	Flat paper	Paper clips	Any surface	Edible

Example Innovation: A sculptural metal core combination pen and scanning device with a spongy finger-size cover with ports for connectors and 4 GB memory, which custom-adjusts for different-size fingers.

Models

A model is a visual description of an idea, theory, or system that accounts for its known or inferred properties and may be used for further study of its characteristics.[40]

A number of disciplines use models as a regular part of their insight-generation processes. In a study of the working methods of great scientists and mathematicians, Dr. Jacques Hadmard found their thinking processes were characterized not by language or standard mathematical symbols but by visual imagery.[41] Albert Einstein is a prime example of this premise, as he has written: "The words of the language, as they are written or spoken, do not seem to play any role in my mechanisms of thought. [After the associations are made visually,] conventional words . . . have to be sought laboriously . . . in a second stage, when the mentioned associative play is sufficiently established . . ."[42]

While models are often used in the financial aspects of business for forecasting and accounting principles, they are used more haphazardly in other areas, such as sales, marketing, and strategy. Andy Grove, former CEO of Intel, found models to be a crucial component of Intel's success: "The model doesn't tell you what the answer is. But it gave us a common language and common way to frame the problem."[43]

In the arena of strategic thinking, models provide the greatest number of insights in the shortest time and using the least space. Compare the two descriptions of strategy in the medical device arena on page 74, the first using a narrative and the second using a model (Figure 3.6).

It's evident, using this example, how much more quickly we can grasp insights using a visual model compared to a narrative. Models give groups a focus on the most relevant issues and provide a common language with which to discuss the business. Author Baruch Fischhoff provides some practical advice about models: "Creating a model is not magic. It takes primarily a commitment to confronting and thinking clearly about the issues. Much of the utility of modeling is extracted from the process itself—putting a team of managers into a room for a day to haggle over the issues. Better to identify now what you don't know than to wait and find out."[44]

Models also act as an objective means of discussing controversial topics when people have taken emotional positions. The model moves the conversation from an intangible thought to a tangible format. For example, "I think . . ." to "here's what the situation looks like in the model on the flip chart." Using models is often a politically savvy move because it provides a shield to the individual and places the issues center stage. There are dozens of effective models. The key is to select the most appropriate models and ensure that they cover the four areas of business: market, customers, competitors, and the company. A common mistake is for a manager to select a few models that focus on only one or two areas—such as customers

Figure 3.6 Strategy Profile

Narrative

TechnoStar has built its advantage by heavily investing limited resources in research and development activities, while CostAlert and CustoSolution have not invested nearly as heavily in R&D. To complement their strategy of premier technology, TechnoStar has also built strong offerings in education and marketing influence to ensure the premium brand status and the higher prices that go along with it. Meanwhile, CustoSolution has chosen to invest heavily in specialized consulting services to provide customers with tailored solutions. To execute their high-end, customized consulting solutions, they have created the largest sales force in the industry with business and clinical experts who can design commercial and medical solutions to their biggest challenges. CostAlert has adopted the strategy of scaling down the offerings of product and service to the bare minimum, while providing a more-competitive price to induce cost-conscious customers to give CostAlert's offerings strong consideration.

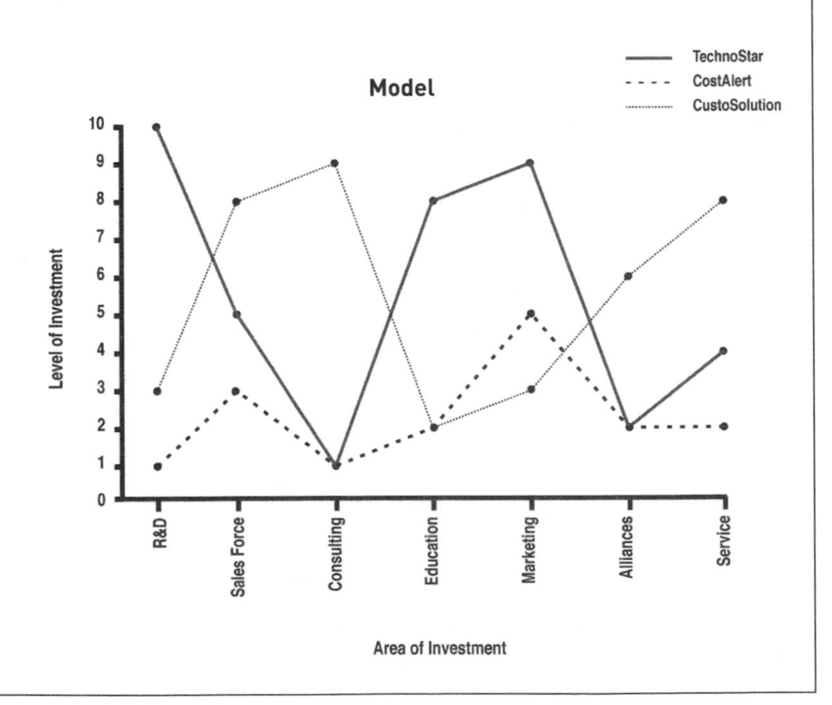

and competition—unknowingly neglecting other critical areas—such as the market and the company—that may generate the real breakthrough insights.

A common mistake is for a manager to select a few models that focus on only one or two areas—such as customers and competition—unknowingly neglecting other critical areas—such as the market and the company—that may generate the real breakthrough insights.

The StrategySphere System helps eliminate these errors by conveniently packaging the top forty strategic thinking models into an online software program. The models are grouped into the four areas of business to help managers ensure that they are covering all the bases. For more information on the StrategySphere System, visit www.strategyskills.com.

EIGHT STRATEGIC THINKING MODELS

The following eight models provide examples in the four areas of market, customers, competitors, and the company (two in each area). A brief description of each model is accompanied by a graphic to provide both the information and the example necessary to apply it to the business. The models use the following three fictitious medical device companies to provide real-world examples:

- TechnoStar—the product leader based on innovative technology.
- CostAlert—the provider of the lowest-cost products.
- CustoSolution—developer of customized solutions.

These fictitious companies represent the three different value disciplines and provide an excellent means of applying the models to players in any industry.

Market Models

In order to understand the full context of your business, it's important to examine what's going on around you. A useful way to do so is to begin the strategic thinking process with a discussion of market models, which sheds light on the macro-environment in which you run your business.

PEST Analysis

A logical place to begin the market review is with a discussion of the PEST—political, economic, social, and technological—factors influencing the business. These four categories enable one to capture key elements swirling about the business and better prepare for their effects.

The PEST Analysis shown in Figure 3.7 is for the medical device arena in which the three fictitious companies play.

The PEST Analysis can be created by dividing the headings into four columns and placing input under each. After the initial

Figure 3.7 PEST Analysis

Political	Economic
1. Legislation on nurse-to-patient ratios 2. FDA-mandated use of bar codes on products 3. JCAHO requirements	1. Employers passing greater share of healthcare costs to employees 2. Retirement of Baby Boomers and their effect on Medicare 3. Group Purchasing Organization's increasing power to lower prices
Social	**Technological**
1. Heightened consumer knowledge of medical issues and treatment options 2. Media's negative portrayal of the healthcare industry 3. Healthcare facilities being qualitatively and quantitatively evaluated on treatment rates	1. Industry moving toward RFID technology 2. Hospital looking for connectivity among drugs, medical devices, monitoring systems, and records 3. Move toward smaller, cross-platform devices

lists are developed, go back and eliminate the factors that are not significant in the overall scope of the business.

Five Forces of Competition

Introduced by Harvard Business School professor Michael Porter, this model assesses the environment and industry structure based on five factors that have the most effect on the business's profitability. In completing the model, it is helpful to rate each of the five factors as "Low," "Medium" or "High," and to record relevant comments next to each. Here are the Five Factors of Competition, along with the key elements for determining the effect of each.

1. Barriers to entry
   - Economies of scale
   - Product differentiation
   - Brand equity
   - Switching costs
   - Capital requirements
   - Intellectual capital
2. Power of buyers
   - Number of key customers
   - Number of alternative sources
   - Customers' switching costs
   - Customers' profitability
   - Threat of backward integration
3. Substitutes
   - Availability of close substitutes
   - Users' switching costs
   - Substitute price-value

4. Power of Suppliers
   - Number of key suppliers
   - Number of substitutes for suppliers' products
   - Suppliers' contribution to quality/service
   - Threat of forward integration
5. Industry Competition
   - Concentration of competitors
   - Industry growth
   - Product differentiation
   - Strategic stakes

Figure 3.8 illustrates the Five Forces of Competition Analysis for the medical device arena in which TechnoStar, CostAlert, and CustoSolution play.

Note the following market insights:

- The threat of new entrants is medium, due to the proprietary technology requirements.
- The bargaining power of buyers is high because of growing pricing transparency.
- The threat of substitute products is medium, and nontraditional players with disruptive technologies need to be monitored.
- The bargaining power of suppliers is high because they are also working with consumer electronics firms that offer substantially higher revenue than do the medical device companies.
- Industry competition is high among the three primary players and smaller secondary players.

Simply going through the motions and checking off a box that says you've finished the model is a waste of your team's time. Listing

Figure 3.8 Five Forces of Competition

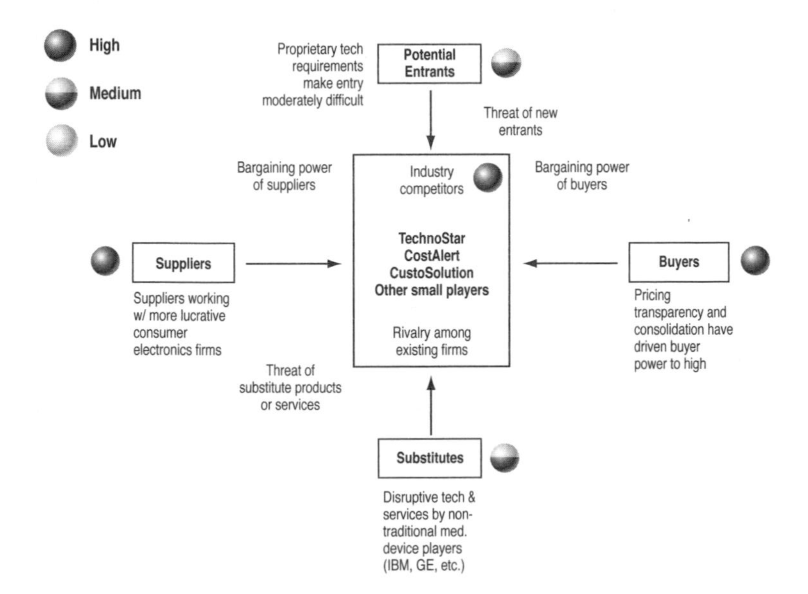

the insights generated from your work on the model ensures that the exercise breathes new thinking into your business. A model without insights is nothing more than lines on paper.

Customer Models

Customers are at the heart of any business. Since they are so near and dear, we tend to take thinking deeply about them for granted. That is, until one day they up and leave. Then we pull the team together and ask the collective "What happened?" To keep your current customers and gain new ones, there are several models you can use to make sure the heart of your business keeps beating.

Business Driver Matrix

The Business Driver Matrix is designed to evaluate the attributes of the business based on two parameters: relevance to customers (Low to High) and differentiation from competitors (Low to High). An

Figure 3.9 Business Driver Matrix

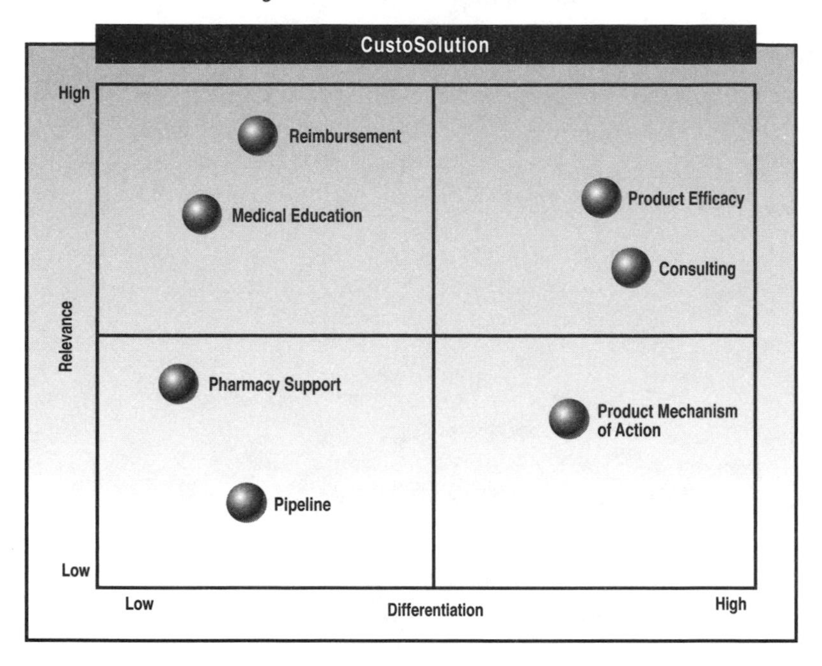

attribute is an inherent quality or characteristic of the business (e.g., product efficacy, customer service, etc.). Figure 3.9 is an example of a Business Driver Matrix for CustoSolution.

From the example, it can be seen that product efficacy and consulting are the two attributes customers highly value and are significantly differentiated from the competition. The model can be used to understand where to allocate resources either to increase an offering's relevance to customers or to enhance its differentiation from competitors' offerings. Using the model to determine which attributes should receive fewer resources in the future can also help you make strategic trade-offs.

Value Factor Analysis

The VFA (Value Factor Analysis) model developed by Dr. Curtis Carlson, together with Dr. William Wilmot of the University of Montana, provides a quantitative estimate of the value of a particular business offering to a customer group versus offerings of the competition.[45] VFA provides a breakdown of value by individual attributes to give decision makers a way to assess the trade-offs involved. Since you can use benefits or costs to determine value, the VFA model uses "Quality" and "Convenience" as the two benefit categories and costs for the denominator. Figure 3.10 is an example of the VFA model.

To create the model, fill in your product or service in the column to the immediate right of "Customer Importance" and as many as three competitors in the other columns. Identify the key quality attributes that would factor into the customer's evaluation of the product/service and enter them under the "Quality" column. For each quality attribute, determine its importance to the customer from 0–5, with 0 being no importance and 5 being high importance, and list it under the "Customer Importance" column. For each offering, record how well it satisfies the customer on that quality attribute using a 0–5 scale, with 0 being lowest and 5 being highest. The Benefit for each offering is calculated by multiplying the Customer Importance by Satisfaction.

Repeat this process for "Convenience" and "Cost." (One note on the "Cost" section: a higher cost to the customer means a higher number for the "Expense" column; for example, a high base price of an automobile would be a high expense number, that is, a 4 or 5.)

Total the Benefits columns for each of the offerings for Quality and Convenience by adding the scores. Total the Cost columns for each of the offerings by adding their scores. To calculate the value factor for each competitor, multiply their Quality Benefits total by their Convenience Benefits total, and then divide that number by the Total Cost Benefits number.

For a company's product or service to have discernible value, a value factor of two to ten times greater than the competition is required. The model is an effective way to break down an offering into its individual components and analyze them at a granular level. While

Figure 3.10 Value Factor Analysis

Quality	Customer Importance	TechnoStar		CustoSolution		CostAlert	
		Satisfaction	Benefit	Satisfaction	Benefit	Satisfaction	Benefit
Device Material	3	5	15	3	9	2	6
Medical Education	1	2	2	3	3	1	1
Consulting	4	3	12	5	20	1	4
Clinical Data	3	4	12	3	9	2	6
Clinical Experience	5	4	20	3	15	3	15
Total Quality Benefits			61		56		32

Convenience	Customer Importance	TechnoStar		CustoSolution		CostAlert	
		Satisfaction	Benefit	Satisfaction	Benefit	Satisfaction	Benefit
Size of Device	4	5	20	3	12	2	8
Procedure Time	5	4	20	3	15	2	10
Ordering	2	2	4	3	6	2	4
Sales Support	3	2	6	3	9	1	3
Total Convenience Benefits			50		42		25

Cost	Customer Importance	TechnoStar		CustoSolution		CostAlert	
		Expense	Cost	Expense	Cost	Expense	Cost
Device Price	5	5	25	3	15	2	10
Disposable Price	3	4	12	3	9	1	3
Training Time	2	3	6	3	6	2	4
Total Cost Benefits			43		30		17

Value Factor			71		78		47

it is customary for managers to conduct an initial run of this exercise, it's wise to do customer research to validate the factors in each area (Quality, Convenience, Cost) and the relative importance of each.

Competitor Models

Mention the competition, and it usually evokes an emotional response: "They aren't in our league"; "We have much better people";

"We'd crush them if we had their budgets." Peel back the layer of emotion and what's at the core of your understanding of the competition? Following are several models which give you an objective way to assess the competitive landscape and generate insights into building that elusive competitive advantage.

Competitive Strengths Assessment

The Competitive Strengths Assessment model is used to create a quantitative evaluation of how firms compare to one another on key success factors. Figure 3.11 is a comparison of CustoSolution, TechnoStar, and CostAlert on the key measures of market success.

To create the model, list your firm's product/service across the top row, then as many as three competitors. List the industry's key success factors under the "Measures" column. Assign a weight from 0 to 1 (e.g., .15, .25, .50) to each measure based on its perceived importance in shaping competitive success. Keep in mind that the sum of the weights must total 1. Enter a number in the "Rating" column for the firm and its rivals on each factor using a scale of 1–10, with 1 being low and 10 being high. Multiply the "Rating" by

Figure 3.11 Competitive Strength Analysis

Measures	Weight	CustoSolution		TechnoStar		CostAlert	
		Rating	Score	Rating	Score	Rating	Score
Product Efficacy	.25	7	1.75	9	2.25	5	1.25
Device Size	.20	6	1.2	8	1.6	4	0.8
Clinical Data	.15	6	0.9	7	1.05	3	0.45
Clinical Experience	.10	6	0.6	6	0.6	4	0.4
Base Price	.08	6	0.48	7	0.56	3	0.24
Sales Support	.07	4	0.28	3	0.21	2	0.14
Medical Education	.05	4	0.2	2	0.1	2	0.1
Training	.05	5	0.25	6	0.3	3	0.15
Ordering	.05	6	0.3	3	0.15	4	0.2
Totals	1		5.96		6.82		3.73

the "Weight" for each entry to calculate the "Score." When you have finished rating all competitors on all measures, add the scores to determine their overall competitive strength. The greater the difference between a firm's overall rating and the scores of the competitors, the larger its net competitive advantage.

Strategic Group Map

A Strategic Group Map is developed to visually reveal the competitive positions of industry rivals on the two key criteria that differentiate them from one another. If the industry players are visually close to one another, a circle can be drawn around them to indicate they are part of the same strategic group. Figure 3.12 is an example of a Strategic Group Map.

To construct a Strategic Group Map, first identify two key competitive characteristics (e.g., geographic reach, price) that differentiate firms from one another and label each axis with one. In the example in Figure 3.12, Technology and Service have been identified as the two key differentiating competitive characteristics. Fill in the start and end values (e.g., Low/High) for each axis. Then evaluate each player and plot its position on the map. In this example, the three competitors are distinct enough regarding the two criteria (Technology and Service) that they are not part of the same strategic groups.

The Company Models

While we sometimes get caught up in a competitor's new product launch or a customer's complaint letter, we can often have the greatest positive effect on our business by thoughtfully analyzing ourselves. Objectively looking at our own company and determining what we do well (no, it's not everything) and what we need to do better (yes, it's usually more than two things) can dramatically shape our future success. Using models to analyze our company can

Figure 3.12 Strategic Group Map

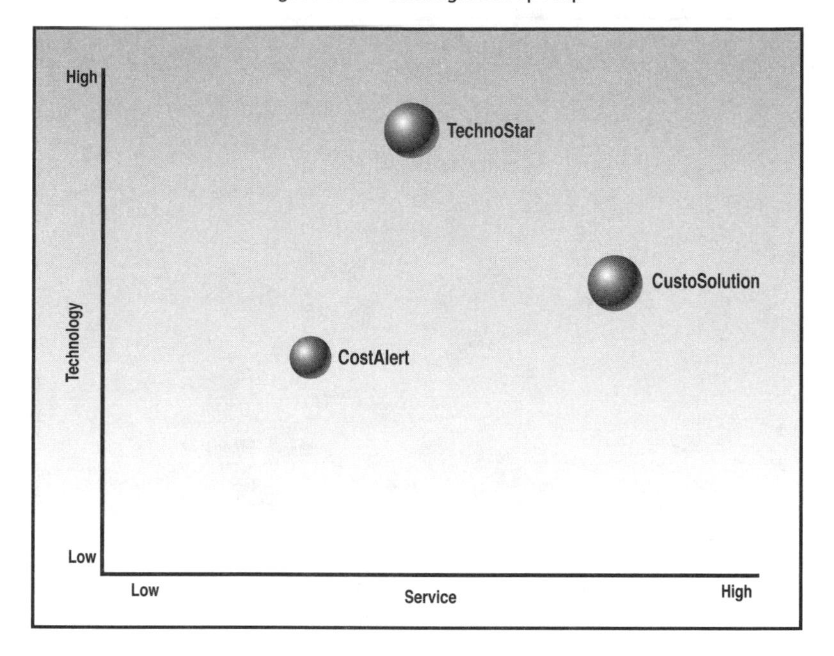

be as painful as looking into a full-length mirror on January 2, but it's necessary for a full picture of our business health.

Opportunity Matrix

An Opportunity Matrix is a valuable method of evaluating resource allocation for the opportunities identified. It provides a logical follow-up exercise to the SWOT Analysis (evaluation of the Strengths, Weaknesses, Opportunities, and Threats), as it takes the opportunities identified and helps a manager prioritize them. It enables an effective allocation of resources by prioritizing opportunities based on two criteria: probability of achievement and impact on the business. Figure 3.13 is an Opportunity Matrix for CustoSolution.

To create an Opportunity Matrix, use the opportunities identified in your company's SWOT Analysis. For each opportunity, determine the probability of achieving the opportunity on a scale of 1–10, with 1 being lowest and 10 being highest, and the impact on the business

Figure 3.13 Opportunity Matrix

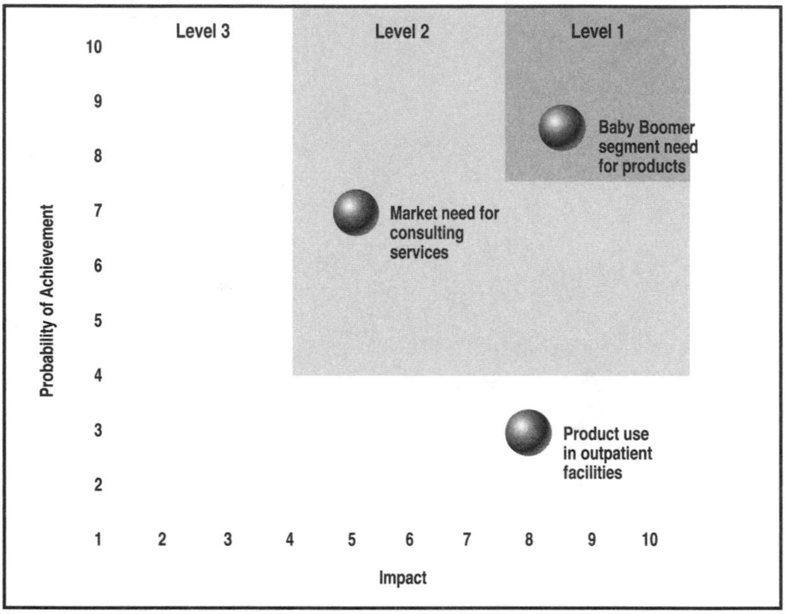

if the opportunity is achieved (using the same 1–10 scale). Based on this evaluation, place the opportunity on the appropriate place on the map. Repeat the process for each additional opportunity.

Once the model is completed, opportunities will fall into one of three levels, based on probability of achievement and impact on the business. Opportunities in Level I should be given strong consideration for a disproportionate share of resources, while those in Levels II and III less so. However, as strategic thinking blends art and science, there may be opportunities in Level III that you believe deserve greater resources, even though the likelihood of success is less. Those are the decisions managers must come to grips with and why a spreadsheet alone has never been enough to determine the most effective strategy. The same exercise can also be run using "threats" (Threat Matrix), with the only change being the label of the Y-axis to "Probability of Occurrence" (as one is obviously not trying to "achieve" threats).

SWOT Alignment

The SWOT Alignment model aligns the internal capabilities (strengths and weaknesses) with the external possibilities (opportunities and threats) to methodically develop potential strategies. It takes the essence of the SWOT Analysis and answers the question, So what? Based on the strengths, weaknesses, opportunities, and threats, what should the manager do? Figure 3.14 represents a SWOT Alignment model for CustoSolution.

To construct the SWOT Alignment model, list the strengths, weaknesses, opportunities, and threats in their respective boxes. Then create potential strategies by methodically aligning the strengths and opportunities, strengths and threats, weaknesses and opportunities, and weaknesses and threats in the appropriate boxes. This model serves as an appropriate exercise after a SWOT Analysis and Opportunity & Threat matrices have been completed.

Figure 3.14 SWOT Alignment

Internal / External	**Strengths** 1. Customer knowledge 2. Established base of contracts 3. Breadth of portfolio	**Weaknesses** 1. Marketing resources 2. Siloed approach to growth 3. R&D investment level 4. Timely resolution of quality issues
Opportunities 1. Product use in outpatient facilities 2. Baby Boomer need 3. Expansion of consulting services	**Possible Strategies** 1. Leverage customer knowledge to drive consulting services in outpatient facilities	**Possible Strategies** 1. Apply limited marketing resources to the high-growth segment of outpatient facilities
Threats 1. Competitor partnerships w/ nontraditional players 2. Increasing power of buyers 3. Customers awarding non-exclusive agreements	**Possible Strategies** 1. Build in value-added items (i.e., leadership training) to the established base of contracts to add switching costs that prevent greater use of nonexclusive agreements	**Possible Strategies** 1. Create cross-functional SWAT team to speedily address issues from key customers

DIVE MASTER PRACTICE

Select one model from each of the four business components: market, customers, competitors, and the company. Complete the four models for your business. What insights did you generate from each model? What information are you lacking that would help you more completely work through the models? Now, gather several colleagues and work through the models as a group. What insights was the group able to generate? Who else in the organization would add valuable input to these models?

PEARLS OF INSIGHT

- **Insight is the product of two or more pieces of information combined in a unique way.**
- **There are four primary sources of insight that can be mined to further enhance one's acumen:**
    1. Context
    2. Customers
    3. Questions
    4. Models
- **Context is the circumstances in which an event occurs; a setting.**
- **There are three pitfalls of context to avoid in order to be successful:**
    1. Annual Assessment
    2. Relative versus Absolute Performance
    3. Prescription without Diagnosis
- **Three tools that can be used to effectively gauge the context of the business:**
    1. Strategy Tune-up Sessions
    2. OODA Loop
    3. Contextual Radar

- **Customers can verbally provide insight on current offerings, but not future ones.**

- **Observing customers' behavior can provide insight into future offerings.**

- **Three effective question techniques to generate insights:**
    1. Creative Insight Generation Process
    2. SCAMPER
    3. Innovation Box

- **A model is a visual description of an idea, theory or system that accounts for its known or inferred properties and may be used for further study of its characteristics.**

- **It is important to use models to generate insights in the four areas of a business (examples of models in each area in parentheses):**
    1. Market (PEST Analysis & Five Forces of Competition)
    2. Customers (Business Driver Matrix & Value Factor Analysis)
    3. Competitors (Competitive Strengths Assessment & Strategic Group Map)
    4. Company (Opportunity Matrix & SWOT Alignment)

CHAPTER 4

DISCIPLINE #2: ALLOCATION—USING OUR AIR WISELY

When beholding the tranquil beauty and brilliancy of the ocean's skin, one forgets the tiger heart that pants beneath it; and would not willingly remember that this velvet paw but conceals a remorseless fang.

—Herman Melville, novelist and poet

The second discipline of strategic thinking is allocation. Once insights have been generated through the acumen discipline, you have the key ingredient for making resource allocation decisions. Recall that the definition of strategy begins with "the intelligent allocation of limited resources . . ." Resource allocation is at the core of strategy. Discussions of strategy boil down to how to allocate limited resources to maximize business potential. As John McGee, professor of Strategic Management at Warwick Business School, succinctly put it, "Variety within an industry is the result of the different investment decisions of firms taken in the pursuit of competitive advantage."[1]

This anecdote from an assistant comptroller of a large manufacturing company provides a glimpse into the power of resource allocation decisions to influence strategy.

> I received for editing a capital request from the division for a large chimney. I couldn't see what anyone could do with just a chimney, so I flew out for a visit. They've built and equipped a whole new plant on expense orders. The chimney is the only indivisible item that exceeded the $50,000 limit we put on the expense orders. Apparently, they learned informally that a new plant wouldn't be favorably received and since they thought the business needed it, and the return would justify it, they built the damn thing. I don't know exactly what I'm going to say.[2]

While it's one thing to have a neatly written strategy on paper, the truth is the actual or realized strategy of an organization is a result of the resource allocation decisions made by managers each day. When these decisions are made based on information (tip of the iceberg) rather than insights (subsurface iceberg), they will tend toward the status quo and lack innovation. Just as divers need to continually monitor their breathing and remaining oxygen, so too do managers need to continually gauge their resource levels. Therefore, it is critical to have a firm understanding of resource allocation and how to maximize its potential for your organization.

THREE TYPES OF RESOURCES

Resources can consist of a spectrum of things, depending on the company and the industry in which they compete. Generally, there are three categories of resources:

1. Tangible: Physical assets and financial resources

2. Intangible: Culture, brand, and reputation
3. Human: Knowledge, competencies, and skills

Many managers believe that with an increase in their tangible resources (especially budget), domineering success is inevitable. An example from Major League Baseball quickly disproves this theory. For the past eight seasons, the New York Yankees, under the direction of general manager Brian Cashman, have had a monstrous advantage over their competitors in the key resource—payroll. In 2007, the salaries of playoff teams were as follows: New York Yankees, $207 million, Boston Red Sox, $143 million, Cleveland Indians, $61 million, Colorado Rockies, $54 million, and Arizona Diamondbacks, $52 million. Ironically, in the 2007 playoffs, the Cleveland Indians knocked off the New York Yankees despite having $146 million less to spend on players.[3] In fact, for eight consecutive seasons (2001–2008), the New York Yankees and their gigantic payroll have failed to win the World Series. This is one reason strategy's definition of "the intelligent allocation of limited resources . . ." rings so true on and off the field.

Too often, lip service is paid to the importance of intangible resources. Discussions of strategy and building competitive advantage tend to gravitate toward the tangible budget dollars that are battled over year in and year out. While companies such as Virgin, Southwest Airlines, and Four Seasons Hotels and Resorts are repeatedly recognized as those lucky few who have built their success on such intangibles as culture and brand, most companies simply breeze past the opportunity to fully explore the benefits intangible resources provide.

Interestingly, hard data have been developed to show the value of soft resources. Research by Aswath Damodaran, a professor in the Stern School of Business at New York University, calculated just how valuable intangible resources could be. In his examination of Coca-Cola, he found that 89 percent of the company value is directly attributed to the brand—an intangible worth billions and billions of dollars.[4]

When it comes to human resources, talent and time figure prominently. Talent is the personnel that provide the intellectual firepower in the form of knowledge and skill sets. While talent is also visible, the knowledge and skills behind it are not. In fact, one of the challenges many groups face is how to effectively share knowledge across functional groups, business units, and geographic locations. Designing tools and vehicles to collect, record, and share insights is a critical activity in today's knowledge-driven environment.

How an individual, group, or organization spends its time is the least tangible of the three resource categories, and potentially the most important. Companies attempt to influence how their employees spend their time using mechanisms such as action plans, activity reports, and time sheets. While these measures appear to provide some degree of control, how many precious hours, days, and years are spent on the urgent, yet unimportant, activities that consume the most time? Professor Robert Kaplan of Harvard Business School offers the following observations: "I have recommended to many leaders that they track how they spend each hour of each day for one week, then categorize the hours into types of activities: business development, people management, and strategic planning, etc. For most executives, the results of this exercise are startling—even horrifying—with obvious disconnects between what their top priorities are and how they are spending their time."[5]

> How an individual, group, or organization spends its time is the least tangible of the three resource categories (tangible, intangible, and human), and potentially the most important.

In order for resources to be a key component in successful strategy, four criteria need to be met:

1. Replication difficulty: the resource is challenging for others to copy.
2. Value generation: the resource must lead to superior value for the customer.
3. Sustainability: the resource is plentiful enough to be used repeatedly.
4. Lack of substitutes: the resource cannot be readily substituted by another resource that performs a similar function.

Consider Cirque du Soleil and the success they have earned since the company was founded in 1984 with just twenty street performers. Today, Cirque has more than thirty-five hundred employees representing forty nationalities and revenue of more than $600 million. A brief examination of their primary resources on the four criteria for resource success in strategy yields the following:

1. Replication difficulty: Performers are elite athletes who, in most cases, just miss making their national teams in sports such as gymnastics and dance. These athletes have the motivation of still trying to prove themselves, and they are limited in number. The creative genius of Cirque's founder Guy Laliberte is also difficult to copy, as he has built a formidable team of designers, artists, and musicians who work relentlessly to transform his vision into reality.
2. Value generation: The high-caliber performers working in a sophisticated artistic format create a unique entertainment experience for adults that is proven in the upper-echelon ticket prices that feed the sold-out shows traveling to one hundred cities on four continents.
3. Sustainability: The performers' world-class conditioning allows them to work night after night at exceedingly high levels. Celine Lavallee, Cirque's head talent scout, has created a global network of contacts to continuously feed new

acts into the system. As a sample, the database of global performers includes giants, whistlers, contortionists, pickpockets, skateboarders, clowns, and dislocation artists.

4. Lack of substitutes: Cirque walks a fine line between finding truly unique artists (an Argentinian opera singer standing seven feet tall and weighing four hundred pounds) and being able to find replacements to fill roles. While other performance troupes and the traditional circuses have attempted to enter Cirque's market space with similar offerings, the Cirque brand championed by a visionary leader has no match when it comes to the high-level performances developed on a continual basis in premier world locations.

FOCUS

People think focus means saying yes to the thing you've got to focus on. But that's not what it means at all. It means saying no to the 100 other good ideas that there are. You have to pick carefully. I'm actually as proud of many of the things we haven't done as the things we have done.

—Steve Jobs, CEO, Apple

The key to effectively allocating resources resides in the ability to focus. Focus demands the discipline to allocate resources to specific areas and activities rather than spread them evenly across the business. Focus comes from the ability and willingness to make trade-offs. Trade-offs are about choosing one path and not the other, and they involve incompatible activities—more of one thing necessitates less of another. In most industries, you can choose to be the leader in researching and developing new products or the leader in providing low-cost goods, but you cannot do both without bearing major inefficiencies.

Making trade-offs is one of the most difficult tasks for managers, and they rarely make them. Instead, they hedge their bets and try to be everything to everyone. Therefore, good leaders cannot afford to be like Farmer Brown, who hops on his tractor and spreads fertilizer evenly across the crops in hopes that everything will grow. If leaders spread their resources evenly across the business, their business will end up in the same condition as Farmer Brown's fertilizer.

Strategy is as much about what you choose *not* to do as it is about what you choose *to* do. Focus requires trade-offs, and trade-offs require risk. Those leaders who are not willing to take risks will never make it to the top of the strategic summit. Two groups of questions can help you make the trade-offs necessary to focus your resources. Here is the first group of questions.

> Focus demands the discipline to allocate resources to specific areas and activities rather than spread them evenly across the business.

1. Who are we serving?
2. What are we offering?
3. How are we offering it?

Most managers do a relatively good job of answering these questions. What most of us don't do often enough, however, is stop and carefully consider our answers to this second group of questions.

1. Which potential customers are we choosing not to serve?
2. What are we not offering?
3. How will it not be offered?

The process of posing these questions can help accomplish the all-important task of moving resources from unproductive areas to productive ones. Author Richard Koch writes: "Progress requires taking resources from less profitable activities and redeploying them in more profitable ones. The biggest mistake most businesses make is to keep unproductive resources going. The essence of strategy is to identify the most productive activities and throw all your resources behind them."[6]

To borrow a saying from the beer industry, "know when to say when" in deciding the right time to pull resources from ineffective initiatives and apply them elsewhere.

A study conducted by the consulting firm McKinsey & Co. surveyed one thousand global executives on resource allocation. Over the past three years, 23 percent of executives said more than 25 percent of their company's invested capital went to existing underperforming investments they believe should have been terminated.[7] Continuing to invest limited resources in underperforming areas is a result of a lack of strategic thinking. Because strategic thinking consists of generating business insights on a continual basis, it requires an interactive mind-set with the market, customers, competitors, and your own company. A good strategist is constantly monitoring where resources are going and what effect they are having on the business.

An insidious cause of ineffective resource allocation is tied to the motivations of the manager. If the culture of a company is that risks met with failure are punished harshly, managers quickly learn to make decisions that give them the least chance for failure. Unfortunately, this unwillingness to take risks means weak strategy. Strategy always involves calculated risk because of the necessary trade-offs, and risk opens you up to the chance of failure. Professor Michael Beer of the Harvard Business School observes: "Managers tend to commit resources too much or too quickly for schemes (projects, goals) they consider likely to improve current business (and thereby their own personal performance and career interests), while allocating inadequate resources to new opportunities and innovations that could ultimately benefit the whole organization's performance. When this dynamic dominates the decision-making process it becomes detrimental to the organization's long-term effectiveness and performance."[8]

In a perfect world, resources would be allocated in an objective, calculated way, driven by the pursuit of the organization's optimal state. In reality, emotion, financial incentives, and career goals make resource allocation a challenge.

PRUNING THE BUSINESS FOR NEW GROWTH

You will find something more in woods than in books. Trees and stones will teach you that which you can never learn from masters.

—Saint Bernard (1090–1153)

When it comes to strategy, what can be learned from a tree? An apple falling from a tree inspired Sir Isaac Newton's discovery of the law of gravity. And the expression "can't see the forest for the trees" is used to describe managers who are too tactical in nature. Anything else?

If you have trees on your property, you are familiar with pruning, or cutting off branches in order to produce strong, healthy, and attractive trees. It's not a glamorous activity, and it can be overlooked year after year. However, never pruning a tree can result in disease, decay, and stunted or uncontrolled growth. How often are you pruning initiatives, activities, and tactics from your business? Managers in organizations large and small are crying for more resources when they may already have all the resources they need. They just have them tied up in traditional, unproductive tactics that add no value to customers. When every opportunity that walks in the door receives resources, only one word can help: *no.*

Saying no to agenda-less meetings, no to "cc:" e-mails about the new janitor hired in the Birmingham plant, and no to perpetual tactics (e.g., trade show booths that deliver zilch) that haven't been rethought in years is the first step in pruning a business. Continuing to invest limited resources in unproductive activities is akin to gift wrapping market share for your competitors. Unfortunately, human beings aren't big on changing, even if it means life or death.

Dr. Edward Miller, dean of the medical school and chief executive officer of the hospital at Johns Hopkins University, illustrates the point: "If you look at people after coronary-artery bypass grafting two years later, 90 percent have not changed their lifestyle. And that's been studied over and over again. Even though they know they have a very bad disease and they know they should change their lifestyle, for whatever reason, they can't."[9]

Research shows that 95 percent of executives say their companies do not have a rigorous and disciplined process for focusing top management's time on the most important issues.[10] In fact, 50 percent of senior management meetings have either the same agenda from meeting to meeting or take a completely ad hoc approach. When you combine the clinical and business data, they don't paint an optimistic picture of our ability to prune the business.

> Saying no to agenda-less meetings, no to "cc:" e-mails about the new janitor hired in the Birmingham plant, and no to perpetual tactics . . . that haven't been rethought in years is the first step in pruning a business.

Restaurateur Danny Meyer of Union Square Hospitality Group, who founded Gramercy Tavern (#1 in New York according to the Zagat Survey) and Union Square Café (#2 in New York), had this to say on the importance of *no*: "I've made much more money by choosing the right things to say no to than by choosing things to say yes to. I measure it by the money I haven't lost and the quality I haven't sacrificed."[11]

Meg Whitman, former CEO of eBay, echoes those sentiments: "Strategy at eBay is as much about the art of exclusion as it is about deciding what to do. We're blessed with lots of great ideas that we could pursue, but I'm a big believer in focus: Let's do six or eight things at 100 percent as opposed to twenty things at 60 or 70 percent."[12]

While the ability to say no has catapulted Union Square Hospitality Group and eBay to great success, the inability to say no has hamstrung Yahoo. An internal document, titled "The Peanut Butter Manifesto," written by Yahoo senior executive Brad Garlinghouse, denounced how the company had spread its resources too thin. At the time, CEO Terry Semel agreed: "We've got to get back to basics and again zero in on a few key priorities. I looked at the Yahoo flowchart and I saw it had 44 business units and realized neither I nor anyone else could ever manage 44 different business units." He eventually slashed it to four.[13]

According to the USDA (United States Department of Agriculture), the three main reasons for pruning trees are safety, health, and aesthetics.[14] In a business, these translate into the following three pruning pitfalls:

1. Safety: comfortable complacency
2. Health: political consensus
3. Aesthetics: unprofitable growth

Safety: Comfortable Complacency

In the tree world, pruning for safety involves removing branches that could fall and cause injury or damage; trimming branches to preserve sight lines for roads; and removing branches that grow into utility lines. In the cozy confines of conference rooms, safety represents that comfortable complacency of doing the same things in the same ways as they've always been done. Not wanting to jeopardize their next step on the career ladder, managers stay the safest course, creating a culture of complacency until the business unit smashes into the rocks of innovation created by their competitors.

Health: Political Consensus

In the tree world, pruning for health involves removing diseased or insect-infested wood; thinning the crown to increase airflow and reduce pest problems; and removing crossing and rubbing branches. Political consensus within businesses involves self-serving interests (bugs), lack of candid communication (reduced airflow), and differing agendas (crossing branches). In order to keep organizations in a healthy state of balance or stasis (ironically, another word for motionless), many resource allocation decisions are driven by political consensus.

In other words, to protect the self-serving fiefdoms and avoid any turf wars, the trade-offs, pruning, and noes that are essential to growth are drowned in the vanilla-colored sea of mediocrity that seems to emanate from consensus. To quote Steelcase's CEO James Hackett again: "Their goal in formulating a point of view was not to reach consensus; the team didn't want to dilute what it had learned. Consensus is often about finding middle ground, because people want to feel good about their colleagues and maintain friendly relations. This doesn't necessarily lead to the best decision, which was what this team was after."[15]

Be aware that political consensus will be an obstacle in pruning the business. Developing a Person-Position Map that identifies key people, their positions of interest, and decision-making frames is one method of avoiding this pitfall.

Aesthetics: Unprofitable Growth

In the tree world, pruning for aesthetics involves enhancing the natural form and character of trees or stimulating flower production. Unprofitable growth is the proverbial "growth for growth's sake," in which an organization and its executives become mesmerized by the allure of a larger top line. It means an uncontrolled approach to growth that forsakes profit and instead casts an eye for acquisitions that actually wind up destroying value. Harvard Business School professor Michael Porter says: "Among all other influences, the desire to grow has perhaps the most perverse effect on strategy. Trade-offs and limits appear to constrain growth. Serving one group of customers and excluding others places a real or imagined limit on revenue growth. Broadly targeted strategies emphasizing low price result in lost sales with customers sensitive to features or service. Differentiators [intentionally] lose sales to price-sensitive customers."[16]

Saying no through the necessary trade-offs means not serving all customers and all needs. Some managers cannot comprehend not serving a segment of potential customers and leaving money on the table, even if it's killing their business. This ability to say no also means not jumping through every hoop that customers say they need. Again, to quote GE's CEO Jeff Immelt, here is what he said regarding his approach to customers and strategy: "I've spent my lifetime working with customers, and I love customers. I get great insight from them—but I would never let them set our strategy for us. But by talking to them, I can put it in my own language. Customers pay our bills, but they will never pick our people or set our strategies."[17]

According to the USDA, pruning a tree in the dormant season is best for three reasons: to help the pruner see and shape the structure of the tree; to maximize wound closure in the growing season after pruning; and to discourage excessive sap flow from wounds. Translation: It's better to prune activities and resources during the course of "normal" business on a continual basis than to wait until a major crisis. In crisis mode, we are more apt to overreact and narrowly focus cuts on symptoms and not the root causes of the issues. By pruning on a regular basis (monthly, quarterly, or yearly), we can avoid chain saws and stick with pruning shears, providing a better chance at new growth.

PRUNING TOOLS

There are a number of valuable tools to use in pruning activities and tactics for resource allocation. Identifying or base-lining the current resource allocation (including how a manager's time is spent) is a necessary starting point in any analysis. One useful model is the Strategy Profile.

The Strategy Profile

The Strategy Profile is a valuable tool for visualizing strategy on the competitive landscape. It does so by comparing investment levels in resource allocation according to the key areas of industry competition. The Strategy Profile provides insight into three areas:

1. It shows the strategic profile of an industry by depicting the factors that currently affect competition among industry players, as well as those factors that might be influential in the future.
2. It captures the strategic profile of current and potential competitors, identifying which factors they invest in strategically.
3. It draws the company's strategy profile, showing where it invests its resources and how it might invest in them in the future.

Using the Strategy Profile to understand where key market players are investing their resources, and to what level, is an effective means of determining where the true differentiation exists. To construct a Strategy Profile for your business, complete the following steps:

1. List the areas of potential investment under "Industry Factors" in the left column.
2. List the key competitors across the top row.
3. Rate the players for each factor on a scale of 1–10, with 1 being a low investment and 10 being a high investment.

Note that the investments levels are relative to the competitors' levels. Therefore, whichever player has the most sales reps in the industry would receive the highest number. This is the case even though for another competitor it may be its highest absolute investment of resources. The relative investment level is used because the goal of the model is to understand the differences in resource allocation among players, thus showing the differences in strategy.

For the fictitious companies in the example, the three competitors are listed across the top and the areas of investment along the left side. Each player is then rated on its levels of investment for the respective factors using the 1–10 scale (see Figure 4.1).

Next, place the areas of investment along the X-axis. Then plot the scores for each area using different lines/colors for each market player and label them accordingly (see Figure 4.2).

As demonstrated earlier, this figure shows the strategy curves for the three competitors. We see that TechnoStar invests significantly more in R&D, education, and marketing than its competitors; CustoSolution places its biggest investments in service, consulting, and its sales force; and CostAlert has a minimum

Figure 4.1 Strategy Profile—Step 1

	TechnoStar	CostAlert	CustoSolution
R&D	10	1	3
Sales Force	5	3	8
Consulting	1	1	9
Education	8	2	2
Marketing	9	5	3
Alliances	2	2	6
Service	4	2	8

Figure 4.2 Strategy Profile—Step 2

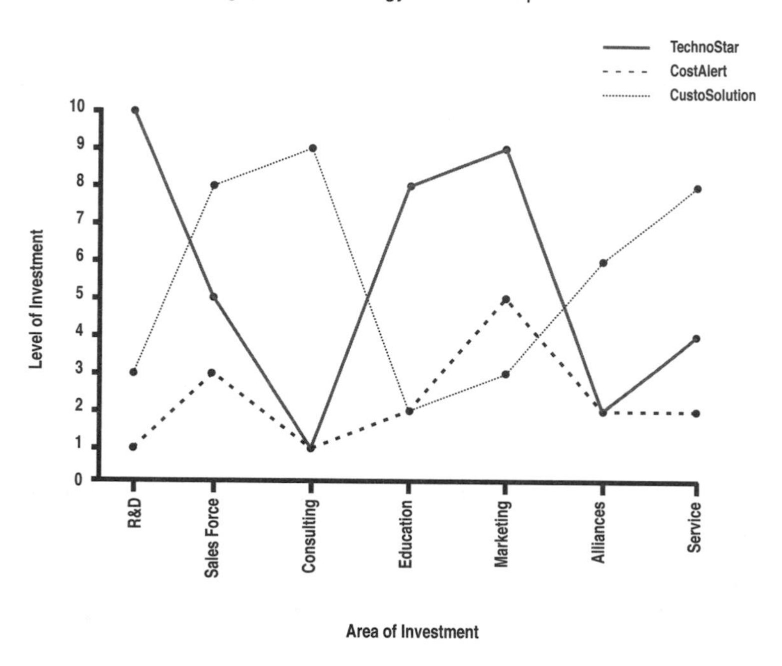

investment across the board, which allows it to maintain lower costs and charge lower prices.

The Trade-off Matrix

An effective follow-up tool to the Strategy Profile is the Trade-off Matrix, which offers a simple means of assessing the strategic trade-offs necessary to create a more-effective strategy. Using the key factors of competition identified in the Strategy Profile, determine which factors should receive no future resources (list in the "Eliminate" quadrant); which factors should receive increased resources (list in the "Increase" quadrant); which factors should receive fewer resources (list in the "Decrease" quadrant); and which factors could be created that the industry has not offered in the past (list in the "Create" quadrant).

Using the earlier example, Figure 4.3 shows the Trade-off Matrix for CustoSolution. The Trade-off Matrix is an effective

Figure 4.3 Trade-off Matrix

CustoSolution

Eliminate	Increase
Alliances	Services Clinical Consulting
Decrease	**Create**
Sales Force	Business Consulting

means of altering your company's future strategy to accentuate the differentiation that customers value in your offerings.

Strategy Filter

Another helpful tool to use in allocating resources and making trade-offs is the Strategy Filter. Consisting of several different models, a Strategy Filter can be an excellent tool to ensure that the members of an organization are making the most of their resources. The Strategy Filter I developed consists of a customized list of criteria that an opportunity, threat, issue, or challenge must meet in order to receive resources in the form of capital, talent, or time. It eliminates emotions and positions from daily discussions and focuses attention on the objective criteria that have already been established. Although a Strategy Filter is a tailored tool, there are nevertheless four main areas to consider as you develop one.

1. Purpose: the mission, vision, and values of the group
2. Business design: the business model on which the group operates, including the context, customer focus, offerings, differentiation, and strategy shield (competitive barriers)
3. Strategy: the overall direction and focus of the group
4. Impact: the qualitative and quantitative effects of channeling resources to the necessary activities

DIVE MASTER PRACTICE

Develop a Strategy Profile for your business. First select the key factors of competition and label them on the X-axis. Then rate your relative level of resource allocation for each factor on a scale of 1 to 10, with 1 being low and 10 being high. Connect the dots to draw your Strategy Profile. Now rate your closest competitor on its approximate resource allocation for each of the factors of competition. Connect the dots to draw its Strategy Profile. How does your Strategy Profile compare with your competitor's Strategy Profile? Are there significant differences? If so, to whose advantage are the differences? What adjustments can you make to create a more advantageous Strategy Profile?

These four areas establish a clear framework for making resource allocation decisions, and they enable individuals to act in a manner consistent with the intent of the organization. When evaluating an opportunity using the Strategy Filter, a simple rating scale is most effective. The "green light, yellow light, red light" scale is popular since it is commonly understood. A green light indicates the opportunity meets the criteria; a yellow light indicates the opportunity partially meets the criteria; and a red light indicates the opportunity does not meet the criteria.

Strategy's Virtuous Cascade

You know that effective resource allocation is important to business, just as certainly as you know that the fourth piece of deep-dish pizza is going to show up on your waistline. I created Strategy's Virtuous Cascade to help you better understand the benefits of resource allocation (see Figure 4.4).

Figure 4.4 Strategy's Virtuous Cascade

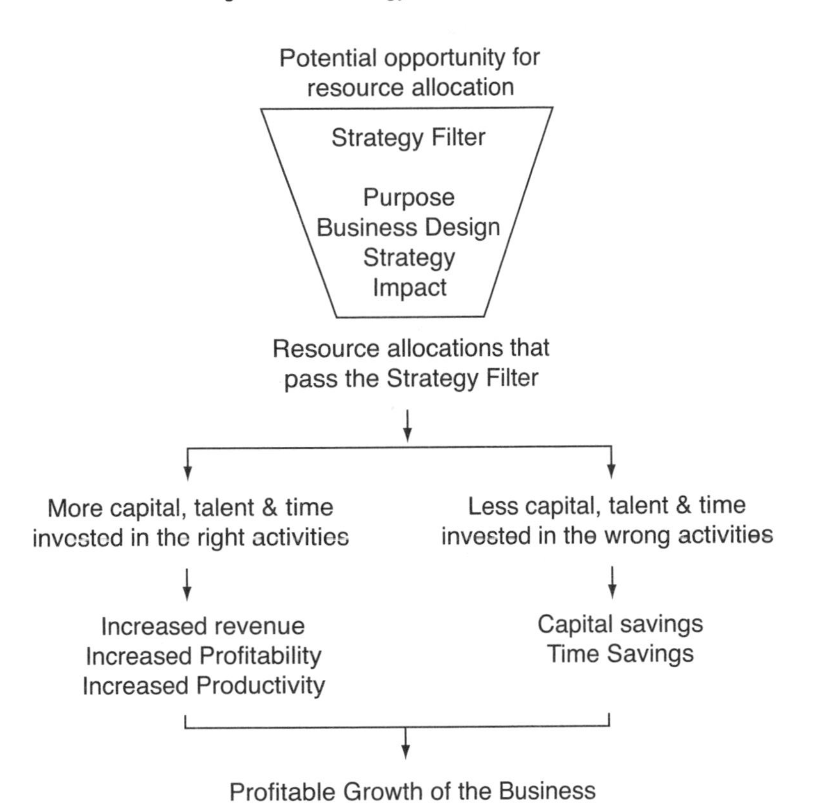

Strategy's Virtuous Cascade shows that when you have properly screened opportunities, threats, and areas for potential resource allocation (using a Strategy Filter), a greater investment in capital, talent, and time is made in the right activities. This investment in the right activities (those congruent with the organization's purpose, business design, overarching strategy, and desired impact) leads to increased revenue (doing the right things), increased profitability (in the right way), and increased productivity (by the right people).

On the flip side, proper resource allocation also means an investment of less capital, talent, and time in the wrong activities, which leads to capital savings (less poor investment) and time savings (less time spent on non-value-driven activities). The result of enhanced resource allocation using the Strategy Filter—and validated by Strategy's Virtuous Cascade—is the profitable growth of your business. A final thought on allocation, the second discipline of strategic thinking: In a society driven to excess by advertising and entertainment designed to fuel the hunger for more of everything, it is paradoxically *less* that is important. In one of the first writings on strategy in history, Lao Tzu, the Father of Taoism, elegantly describes my belief that allocation's core premise is *less is more.*[18]

> Once grasp the great form without a form
> and you will roam where you will
> with no evil to fear,
> calm, peaceful, at ease.
> The hub of the wheel runs upon the axle.
> In a jar, it is the hole that holds water.
> So advantage is had
> from whatever there is;
> but usefulness rises
> *from whatever is not.*

PEARLS OF INSIGHT

- **There are three categories of resources:**
  1. Tangible—Physical assets and financial resources
  2. Intangible—Culture, brand, reputation
  3. Human—Knowledge, competencies, and skills

- **In order for resources to be a key component in successful strategy, four criteria need to be met:**
  1. Replication difficulty—the resource is challenging for others to copy.
  2. Value generation—the resource must lead to superior value for the customer.
  3. Sustainability—the resource is plentiful enough to be used repeatedly.
  4. Lack of substitutes—the resource cannot be readily substituted by other resources that perform a similar function.

- **Focus demands the discipline to allocate resources to specific areas and activities, rather than spread them evenly across the business. Focus comes from the ability and willingness to make trade-offs.**

- **Strategy is as much about what you choose not to do, as it is about what you choose to do.**

- **Three pruning pitfalls when it comes to making trade-offs:**
    1. Safety—Comfortable Complacency
    2. Health—Political Consensus
    3. Aesthetics—Unprofitable Growth
- **A Strategy Filter consists of a customized list of criteria that an opportunity, threat, issue, or challenge must meet in order to receive resources.**
- **While a Strategy Filter is a tailored tool, there are four areas to consider in developing one:**
    1. Purpose—the mission, vision, and values of the group
    2. Business Design—the business model on which the group operates, including the context, customer focus, offerings, differentiation, and strategy shield
    3. Strategy—the overall direction and focus of the group
    4. Impact—the qualitative and quantitative effects of channeling resources to the necessary activities

CHAPTER 5

DISCIPLINE #3: ACTION—SWIMMING TO THE SURFACE

> One kernel is felt in a hogshead; one drop of water helps to swell the ocean; a spark of fire helps to give light to the world. None are too small, too feeble, too poor to be of service. Think of this and act.
>
> **—Hannah More, writer and philanthropist**

The third and final discipline of strategic thinking is action. Our sense of importance seems to be tied to how busy we are, which is one of the reasons why cell phones and their earpieces appear to be surgically affixed to some people's heads. Ernest Hemingway wrote, "Never confuse movement with action." In other words, busyness does not equate with business. One of the most famous marketing tag lines in history, belonging to sports equipment marketer Nike, emphasizes this phenomenon: "Just Do It." Strategic thinking, however, requires that we "*First Think It.*"

Wading through the daily swamp of e-mail, voice mail, meetings, and other activities can leave us gasping for time—and air. Overwhelmed by the tsunami of motion, it's common to react with our own flurry of motion, like someone violently struggling to free her- or himself from a riptide, only to be swallowed up faster by it. Action begins at the individual level with the discipline to focus on the important and not the urgent. Having successfully navigated through the first two strategic thinking disciplines, acumen and allocation, you have the direction you need to apply the discipline of action to your business.

STRATEGY EXECUTION

Research shows the need for greater organizational discipline when it comes to action. The Economist Intelligence Unit surveyed senior executives from 197 global companies with sales in excess of $500 million. They reported the following:

> Our survey indicates that on average, most strategies deliver only 63 percent of their potential financial performance. And more than 1/3 of executives placed the figure at less than 50 percent. If management were to realize the full potential of its current strategy, the increase in value could be as much as 60–100 percent.[1]

Often, we assume that once a sound strategy has been formulated, the execution of that strategy will take care of itself. Research seems to indicate otherwise. A survey of more than four hundred companies showed that 49 percent of business leaders report a gap between their organizations' abilities to articulate a strategic vision and their effectiveness in executing that vision. Additionally, 64 percent of executives did not believe their organizations had the abilities to close that gap.[2] Another study conducted by the Economist Intelligence Unit found 57 percent of firms were unsuccessful at executing strategic initiatives over the past three years.[3] However, a thorough understanding of strategy execution—especially its potential pitfalls and tools—to facilitate the action discipline can dramatically increase your company's chance of success.

Around 500 B.C. in China, a king named Ho-Lu read *The Art of War* by Chinese General Sun Tzu. The king called Sun Tzu to his palace to try out his ideas. Sun Tzu agreed and asked to use the king's concubines for an exercise, with one condition: the king must follow Sun Tzu's decisions. Ho-Lu agreed.

Sun Tzu divided the women into two groups and selected the king's two favorite concubines to be the officers. He explained to them the main points of the military exercises. When he finished his explanation, he asked if they understood the rules. They said yes. When he gave the orders, however, all the women started laughing. Sun Tzu said, "If the strategies are not clear and orders not thoroughly understood, it is the commander's fault."

He repeated the instructions. When he gave orders for the second time, the women again started laughing. Sun Tzu said, "If the strategies have been sufficiently explained but are not carried out, it is the fault of the officers." Then he ordered the two concubines in the officer roles to be executed.

The king told Sun Tzu he understood the point of the exercise; it wasn't necessary to carry out the execution. But Sun Tzu reminded the king of their agreement, and the concubines were executed. Then Sun Tzu appointed two other women as the officers and continued the exercises.

This time when he gave orders, the strategies were followed . . . exactly. At this point the king was so depressed by the loss of his two beloved concubines that he didn't want to watch the rest of the exercises. Sun Tzu told the king, "Your majesty likes words but has no courage to carry them out."

Now that's strategy *execution*.

Strategy execution is often overlooked because it doesn't include the exciting off-site meeting at a resort destination or the fanfare of the product launch kickoff. It's the roll-up-your-sleeves, dig into the details, day-in and day-out work that provides the strategy with oxygen. Without good execution, all you are left with is a dead strategy.

FIVE EXECUTION ERRORS AND THEIR REMEDIES

There are five common execution errors: (1) faulty strategy, (2) unclear resource requirements, (3) poor communication, (4) weak accountability, and (5) lack of calibration. Let's look at each one in detail, along with its corresponding remedy.

Execution Error #1: Faulty Strategy

Garbage in . . . garbage out. Before one can successfully execute strategy, an actual strategy must be developed. Some executives scoff at this, claiming that developing strategy is the easy part and executing strategy is the hard part. Wrong! At least until examples like the following from a multibillion-dollar, multinational company stop appearing. Here is what the company lists as three of its strategies: innovate, expand internationally, and attract and retain talent.

After the laughter subsides, realize that this is common. Jack Welch, former CEO of GE, had the following to say when asked whether strategy development or strategy execution was more important: "I don't think it's an either-or."[4] Organizations tend to fall on either end of the strategy development/execution spectrum when in fact success isn't attainable without a significant commitment to both areas. Lose the either/or mentality when it comes to development and execution and you'll be ahead of the game.

Remedy: Recall the ABCs of what strategy is not: aspiration, best practices, and caution. Do a thorough assessment on the initial strategy to ensure that the foundation for execution is built on solid ground. It is also important to educate managers at all levels on strategy and to develop common terminology so the entire organization has its proper bearings.

Error #2: Unclear Resource Requirements

There is a step between strategy development and strategy execution that can be easily overlooked, but if you do overlook it, the result can be fatal to even the best strategies. And that step is a clear and objective assessment of the resources (tangible, intangible, and human) required to carry the strategy to completion. How often do managers sit down and thoughtfully examine exactly what will be required to move the strategic initiative forward? Many managers examine what will be required of their groups, but they fail to take into account the larger strategy ecosystem. Mapping the resource requirements for the entire strategy ecosystem, from suppliers and distributors to other functional teams within the organization, can paint a much clearer picture of what it will take to succeed.

Remedy: The Resource Allocation Calculator (see Figure 5.1) is a tool I created for evaluating whether a strategy has sufficient resources for implementation. The three areas of tangible, intangible, and human resources are assessed on their actual levels and their required levels. If the actual level of resources is greater than the required level of resources for an area, the area is green-lighted. If the actual level of resources is equal to the required level of resources, with no excess for contingencies, the area is yellow-lighted. If the actual

Figure 5.1 Resource Allocation Calculator

Types of Resources	Required Level	Actual Level	Gap
Tangible	$125,000	$140,000	None
Intangible	Relationships with 15 thought leaders	Relationships with 22 thought leaders	None
Human	2 Sales Reps, 1 Surgeon, 1 District Manager	1 Sales Rep, 1 Surgeon, 1 District Manager	1 Sales Rep

level of resources is less than the required level of resources, the area is red-lighted, to indicate a potential danger for successful execution of the strategy. Strategies with red lights are then reviewed to determine whether to acquire additional resources or to move forward as is.

Example
Goal: Increase number of new users for CustoSolution's medical device.
Objective: Achieve a 75 percent penetration rate for high and medium users of such devices in the East Coast region by the end of the fiscal year.
Strategy: Leverage surgeon thought-leaders' successes with the device to create interest among attending physicians at academic hospitals and physicians at community hospitals in reassessing treatment protocols that don't currently prioritize CustoSolution's product.

As you can see in Figure 5.1, the calculations leave us with the following conclusions:

- Tangible resource requirements are met with a surplus of $15,000, so the strategy is green-lighted.
- Intangible resource requirements are met with a surplus of seven relationships with thought leader surgeons, so the strategy is green-lighted.
- Human resource requirements are not met because one additional sales rep is required, so the strategy is red-lighted until further review.

Error #3: Poor Communication

Research out of Harvard has shown that on average, 95 percent of a company's employees are unaware of or do not understand its strategy.[5] This is almost the same as ten out of eleven offensive players on a football team not knowing which play they are going to run after breaking the huddle. Football teams at nearly all levels have playbooks that describe the exact execution (blocking scheme, receiver routes, etc.) required for each play. In the National Football League, coaches spend thousands of hours a year perfecting strategic execution of plays and communicating their strategies to players. In the past year, how much time has your organization devoted to ensuring that employees completely understand the strategy and their role in developing and executing it?

In business, most organizations reside on either end of the execution spectrum, which means they have no execution plans, or they are inundated with plans and metrics for everything in sight. Choosing a few key metrics to monitor strategy's performance is appropriate. Requiring managers to monitor an overwhelming number of metrics creates the same result as a golfer who watches only the leader board and fails to concentrate on hitting the shots.

Perhaps the biggest communication issue is the failure of an organization's leaders at all levels to explain the strategy for each group of workers and ensure that they understand the explanation. This lack of communication is then compounded by incompetently communicating how the strategy will be executed. In research conducted on strategy execution, only 37 percent of executives agreed with the statement "We're good at communicating our strategy to people at all levels in our organization."[6]

Further contributing to this inability to communicate strategy is that strategy is often the exclusive domain of senior executives. A survey by Management Association Consultancies showed that on average, 80 percent of the input for strategy comes from senior executives. Middle managers account for just 20 percent of the input.[7] Ironically, the case can be made that mid-level managers are the most crucial members in the strategy ecosystem. Very often, these executives receive intelligence from the front lines that can significantly influence strategic direction. Based on their awareness, compensation structure, career path, risk tolerance, etc., they will either decide to boldly act on the intelligence by packaging it in the form of a strategic initiative . . . or not. They have the power to kill potentially game-changing strategies without senior management ever knowing the opportunity existed. To quote Harvard Business School professor Bower once more: "The vast majority of ideas . . . 'bubble up' from employees. [Middle managers] must decide which of the ideas bubbling up to them they will throw their weight behind and which they will allow to languish. The middle managers' decisions play a crucial role in the resource allocation process which, in turn, has a primary effect on the definition and implementation of strategy."[8]

> The case can be made that mid-level managers are the most crucial members in the strategy ecosystem. Very often, these executives receive intelligence from the front lines that can significantly influence strategic direction.

Teaching each group of workers how the strategy relates to what they do daily is crucial for strategy execution. A study by Harris Interactive of twenty-three thousand workers showed that 80 percent don't understand how their tasks relate to their organization's goals and strategies.[9] If the overarching corporate or business unit strategy isn't linked to employees' daily activities, the organization will never realize its full potential. It's wasting the momentum that can only be generated by intellectual and emotional capital pulling in one direction.

Remedy: Poor communication is a function of both ineffective and infrequent communication. Have a clear strategy and communicate it—often. Fred Smith, the chairman, CEO, and president of FedEx, recommends the following: "Once we've bought into [our strategy] as a management team, we then communicate that in every way we can think of. We put it in the employee handbooks. We tie our business plans to it. We tie our incentive plans to it. We make sure our employees understand what we're trying to do and why we're trying to do it."[10]

A tool such as the StrategyPrint (shown in Figure 5.2), which is essentially a two-page business blueprint, serves as a real-time strategic action plan for a business. Having seen all too many strategic plans sitting in binders on shelves gathering dust, I developed the StrategyPrint as a convenient tool to help managers use their strategy to drive their daily activities. It can be used to capture the essence of the business and cascade strategic direction throughout the organization. The StrategyPrint solves the challenge of linking strategy development to strategy execution by providing a concise and thorough document that is more functional than the traditional strategic-plan-in-a-binder.

Page one of the StrategyPrint captures key insights for the business regarding the four key components of business: market, customers, competition, and the company. The majority of these insights are developed on a continual basis through sound strategic thinking.

Page two of the StrategyPrint transforms insights into the strategic action plan including the overarching strategy, business drivers, goals, objectives, strategies, and tactics. The result is a common framework that can be used throughout the business to ensure that everyone is following a unified strategic direction. The StrategyPrint embodies the premise "brevity demonstrates mastery." In a time when managers are expected to move at warp speed and communicate instantaneously, the StrategyPrint enables them to quickly and comprehensively convey key aspects of the business to colleagues, boards of directors, employees, or venture capitalists.

Error #4: Weak Accountability

Accountability, especially in large organizations, is severely lacking. Somebody's not performing? Ship him or her to another business unit. It is much easier to move personnel than to fire them in today's overly litigious, hyper–politically correct world where free speech is fine unless you disagree with people who have a louder lobbying voice. Or put these employees on a "plan," code for "we have

Figure 5.2 Example of a Strategy Print for CustoSolution

CUSTOSOLUTION STRATEGYPRINT®

MARKET

STATE

- Market growth is 6%
- No new entrants

TRENDS

- Baby Boomers retiring and impact on Medicare
- Preference for smaller, cross-platform devices
- Heightened consumer knowledge on treatments

MANAGED CARE OVERVIEW

- Group Purchasing Organization's increase in buying power
- Move to non-exclusive contracts

COMPANY

STRENGTHS

- Customer knowledge due to consulting services
- Established base of contracts
- Breadth of product portfolio

WEAKNESSES

- Non-competitive marketing resources (outspent 3:1)
- Siloed approach to growth
- R&D investment level (outspent 5:1)
- Timely resolution of customer quality issues (60 days)

OPPORTUNITIES

- Outpatient facilities product use (25% of market)
- Baby boomer segment (2/3 of patients)
- Expansion of consulting services (75% of current product customers not using)

THREATS

- Competitor partnerships with non-traditional players
- Increasing power of buyers
- Customers awarding non-exclusive agreements (35%)

CUSTOMERS

TOP 10 ACCOUNTS	PRODUCT CHOICE	YTD REVENUE
1. Kaiser	TechnoStar	$ 22,000
2. Northwestern	TechnoStar	$ 12,000
3. Mayo Clinic	CustoSolution	$ 450,000
4. US Gov't.	CostAlert	$ 6,000
5. UCLA	CustoSolution	$ 397,500
6. U of Arizona	TechnoStar	$ 44,000
7. Sloan-Kettering	TechnoStar	$ 0
8. U of Chicago	CustoSolution	$ 285,000
9. U of Texas	CostAlert	$ 8,400
10. Advocate	CustoSolution	$ 77,000

COMPETITORS

	TechnoStar	CostAlert
MARKET SHARE	37.3%	16.7%
STRENGTHS	- R&D investment - Marketing - Technology platform	- Operational effectiveness
WEAKNESSES	- Breadth of product line	- Inferior technology - R&D resources - Marketing platform
CORE MESSAGE	"Cutting-edge technology"	"Cost-effective technology"
PRICE POSITION	High	Low
COMPETITIVE ACTIVITIES	- Customer CEO Roundtable Symposiums - Thought-Leader Training	- Price-cutting in high-volume accounts

CUSTOSOLUTION STRATEGYPRINT®

OVERARCHING STRATEGY

Leverage depth of customer relationships to gain a greater share-of-wallet by complementing product offerings with high-content service offerings, including business process consulting.

CRITICAL SUCCESS FACTORS

- Cross-functional sharing of customer information and insights
- Development of consulting and business process expertise to expand services

AREAS OF INVESTMENT

1. Product innovation—technology enhancements
2. Upgrade skill sets of sales force
3. Clinical & business consulting expertise

KEY METRICS

1. Revenue
2. Units
3. Consulting Engagements
4. Customer share-of-wallet

MISSION

CustoSolution's commitment to a deep understanding of our customer's business enables us to provide hospital systems with a spectrum of products and services to meet their clinical and business needs.

PERSONNEL & PERFORMANCE

- Leadership development for senior executives
- Build strategic thinking capabilities of mid-level management team
- Create communication channels for internal sharing of best practices

GOALS	1. Grow new users of the medical device	2. Sell services to current product customers	3. Enhance key skill sets
OBJECTIVES	1. Achieve a 25% increase in the # of new users by the third quarter	2. Increase revenue-per-client by 20% through the sale of services by year-end	3. Improve profitability 10% by year-end
STRATEGIES	1. Develop a customer conversion program to facilitate product trial	2. Generate awareness of service offerings through consultative selling and needs assessment tools	3. Train managers on strategic thinking capabilities to improve resource allocation decisions
TACTICS	• Conversion materials • Direct mail campaign • Journal advertising	• Train sales force on service offerings • Incentive program for service sales • Direct mail campaign to service decision makers at hospital systems	• Assessment tools to baseline strategic thinking capabilities • Conduct The Strategist Training System for mid-level managers • Distribute Resource Allocation Calculators

GUGGENHEIM MUSEUM

freeloaders that we're afraid to fire so we'll let them suck milk from the corporate bosom for another year or two until they decide to leave on their own, and in the meantime, our other, good employees' morale will sink like a stone."

When it comes to accountability for strategy execution, compensation can be an effective tool. The promise of greater compensation (raise or bonus) and the threat of none (being fired) are strong forces of accountability. However, research out of Harvard Business School has shown that compensation packages of 70 percent of middle managers and more than 90 percent of frontline employees have no link to the success or failure of strategy implementation.[11] If a manager's accountability can be influenced by compensation, it makes sense to leverage that motivation to drive enhanced strategy execution. This is not an easy task by any means, but the results of not executing the strategy (a.k.a. bankruptcy) are a less appealing alternative.

Remedy: For each strategic initiative, create a one-page worksheet that identifies the goals, objectives, tactics, metrics, resource requirements, and person(s) accountable for execution. Also, tie a portion of every employee's compensation to their ability to execute on strategic initiatives within their business units. For those few organizations such as military branches, where compensation isn't as strong a motivator, begin with a close examination of the key motivators (e.g., rank, people responsibility, etc.) and creatively link them to the ability to execute strategy.

Error #5: Lack of Calibration

Here's a news flash: the majority of plans don't go as planned. Market trends shift, customer value drivers change, and competitors introduce new offerings, all with the potential to derail strategy. Therefore, it is critical to have a continuous pulse on the context of the business in order to detect and adapt to changes in a timely manner. That is one of the reasons why viewing strategy as an annual event is so dangerous. If a key change happens a month after the annual strategic planning process is completed, does it really have to take another eleven months before that change is examined and accounted for?

The need for strategy calibration on a regular basis is not exclusive to the senior management team. Jeff Bezos, CEO of Amazon.com, describes his company's approach to calibrating strategy on a continual basis at different levels: "We have a group called the S Team—S meaning 'senior'—that stays abreast of what the company is working on and delves into strategy issues. It meets for about four hours every Tuesday. The key is to ensure that this happens fractally too, not just at the top. The guy who leads Fulfillment by Amazon is making sure the strategic thinking happens for that business in a similar way. At different scale levels it's happening everywhere in the company."[12]

Remedy: Utilize the Strategy Tune-up, a periodic (i.e., weekly, monthly, quarterly) meeting with key personnel for strategy development and execution to review the context of the business. Just as auto shops run diagnostic checkups on vehicles, the Strategy Tune-up conducts a diagnostic checkup on the business.

BUSINESS PLANNING TERMS

The same Harris Interactive study cited earlier revealed that 63 percent of the twenty-three thousand workers didn't have a clear understanding of their organization's goals and why they're trying to achieve them.[13] A primary reason is that the terms *goal*, *objective*, *strategy*, and *tactic*—easily remembered as the acronym G.O.S.T.—are often used incorrectly and interchangeably. This confusion is a direct cause of poor strategy execution. Let's review each.

> **Goal:** A general target What, *generally*, you are trying to achieve.
>
> Example: To become the market share leader.

Objective: Specific outcome desired—What, *specifically*, you are trying to achieve.

Example: Attain a 32 percent market share for product X by the end of the fiscal year.

The acronym SMART provides a helpful reminder for the criteria of an objective: **S**pecific, **M**easurable, **A**chievable, **R**elevant, **T**ime-bound.

Strategy: The resource allocation plan—How, *generally,* to achieve the goals.

Example: Redistribute all print advertising dollars to a PR campaign to highlight the competitor's weak product reliability profile.

Tactic: The tangible activities/items that carry out the strategies—How, *specifically,* to achieve the goals.

Example: Sell sheet, journal ad, training CD-ROM.

Goals and objectives are *what* is to be accomplished. Strategies and tactics are *how* the goals and objectives will be accomplished. The key differences are represented in Figure 5.3.

Since strategy and tactics both address the *how*, they are often used interchangeably. A helpful way to remember the differences is the "Rule of Touch." If it can be physically touched, it is most likely a tactic (sales brochure, CD-ROM, direct mail piece, etc.). If it can't be physically touched (leveraging a specialty sales force with a single product focus), it is most likely a strategy. As Sun Tzu noted in *The Art of War*, "All the men can see the tactics I use to conquer, but what none can see is the strategy out of which great victory is evolved."

Figure 5.3 G.O.S.T. Summary

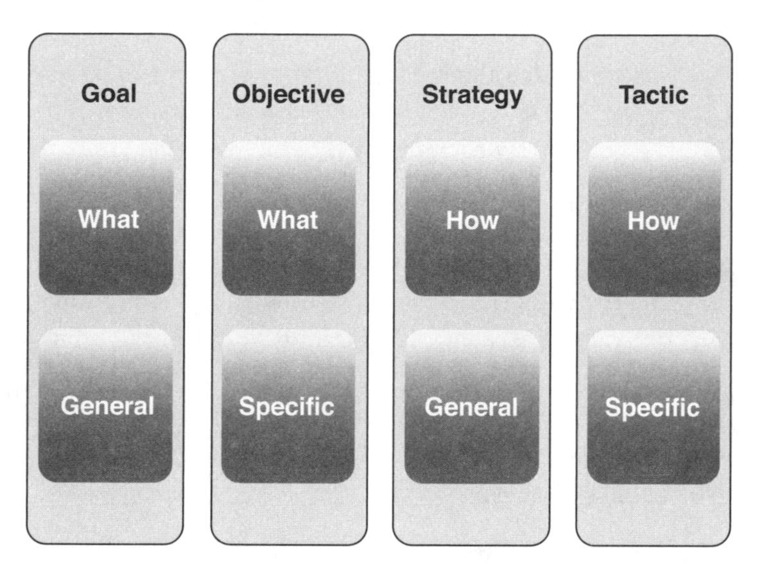

Strategy Formula

Reading maketh a full man, discussion a
ready man and writing an exact man.

—Francis Bacon, English author and philosopher

An architect shows up at the work site of a soon-to-be-constructed, custom-designed home. Gathered around are the numerous subcontractors: construction workers, electricians, plumbers, plasterers, and a host of others. The architect says, "We will be building a five-bedroom, four-bath, contemporary house with cathedral ceilings in the entryway and a three-car garage. Now go to work." Then he gets in his car and drives away. The subcontractors are left scratching their heads because the architect didn't leave any blueprints or written recordings of what they were to do.

DIVE MASTER PRACTICE

Write your top three goals in three separate columns. Below each goal, record the objective that coincides with the goal. Below each objective, write down the strategy you are using to generally achieve the goal and the objective. Below the strategy, identify all the tactics you are investing in to realize the strategy and to achieve the goal and the objective. Is there a consistent and logical flow of thought cascading down from goal to tactics? Do all of the elements meet the criteria described in their respective definitions? Which tactics can be pruned and what tactics should be created to give you a better opportunity for achieving your goals and objectives?

This scene would never happen in the construction field, but it occurs quite frequently in business. Strategies are discussed and directions are given, but in many cases, those strategies are never actually written down. So, some people are working in general directions they vaguely recall, while their colleagues are remembering an entirely different version of the strategy. If a strategy isn't written down, it doesn't exist, at least not in any way that's meaningful to the organization. Does the VP of marketing really have the same concept of the strategy as the VP of R&D, or the VP of sales? If it's not written down, how do you know?

From Mind to Paper

As with many higher-level disciplines—medicine, leadership, and law, for example—transforming an abstract concept such as strategy into a tangible one is part science and part art. The scientific aspect comes from the business acumen required to assess and analyze all the moving parts of a dynamic business. The artistic aspect comes from the need to synthesize the individual elements into a purposeful system of activity that achieves goals and objectives.

The Strategy Formula has been designed to provide managers with the skeletal framework for strategy, much as a wire frame provides sculptors with a base for their works of art. The Strategy Formula ensures that the articulation and communication of strategy are sound and consistent across the business unit, functional groups, or organization as a whole.

As noted earlier, key business planning terms such as goals, objectives, strategies, and tactics (remember G.O.S.T.) are often used interchangeably and incorrectly. The Strategy Formula I developed helps eliminate misuse by guiding the process of channeling strategy from mind to paper.

Strategy Formula = WHAT + HOW + WHO + IMPACT

WHAT: The activity representing the purpose of the strategy.
HOW: The general means or method of accomplishing the strategy.
WHO: The audience the strategy is designed to reach.
IMPACT: The desired result of developing and executing the strategy.

A strong Strategy Statement will address each of these four areas: *What, How, Who,* and *Impact*. Is this the only way a strategy can be written? No. But it does provide a helpful guideline to create common and shared understandings of how strategy can be articulated.

What follows is an example of the Strategy Formula in action in the medical device arena. The Strategy Statement appears first, and then is broken down using the Strategy Formula to see if it contains the four necessary components.

Strategy Statement: Objectively determine which customers to acquire and which customers not to acquire by developing and implementing a proprietary Customer Selection Criteria System to enable the sales force to more effectively allocate their resources and enhance the division's profitability.

Using the Strategy Formula, we identify the four components:

- WHAT: "Objectively determine which customers to acquire and which customers not to acquire . . ."
- HOW: ". . . by developing and implementing a proprietary Customer Selection Criteria System . . ."
- WHO: ". . . sales force . . ."
- IMPACT: ". . . to more effectively allocate their resources and enhance the division's profitability."

Together, the Strategy Statement and Strategy Formula ensure that managers are correctly formulating strategy in order to maximize the subsequent execution. Beware the architect without a blueprint and the manager without a StrategyPrint (the business equivalent): the former is homeless and the latter may soon be.

ACTIVITY SYSTEM MAP

Sustainable advantage comes from systems of activities that are complementary. These "complementarities" occur when performing one activity gives a company not only an advantage in that activity, but also provides benefits in other activities.

—Michael Porter, professor, Harvard Business School

Successful strategy execution depends on a large system of interacting components including personnel, culture, structure, competition, priorities, etc. To that end, an effective model to facilitate successful strategy execution is the Activity System Map, a visual representation of an organization's strategy and the tactics that support it. It provides a thirty-thousand-foot view of the business by capturing the strategy and tactics, and the relationships between the two, on a single page. Designing an Activity System Map first requires the individual to step back and view the business from the high ground to better understand the strategic composition. It then drills down to assemble a conceptual framework, identifying the interrelationships and competencies of the key facets of the business. Once completed, the Activity System Map provides a clear and concise picture of the business, which enables leaders to more effectively set direction and allocate resources.

The Activity System Map consists of the strategic themes of the organization represented by large spheres, and the individual activities or tactics represented by small spheres. Between three and five strategic themes are appropriate to cover the primary hubs of strategy for a business. In addition to identifying the individual strategic themes and tactics, the Activity System Map highlights the strength of the relationships between the strategy and tactics. A solid line between two spheres indicates direct support and a dotted line indicates indirect support.

The Activity System Map for CustoSolution is demonstrated in Figure 5.4. The three strategic themes for CustoSolution are business expertise, customized services, and grassroots marketing, all represented by large spheres. The activities and tactics supporting each of those strategic themes are shown as the smaller spheres clustered around the strategic themes they support.

The following is a list of the steps involved in designing an Activity System Map:

1. Identify and plot three to five strategic themes.
2. Attach tactics that are currently being employed.
3. Add tactics that would strengthen strategic themes.

Figure 5.4 Activity System Map—CustoSolution

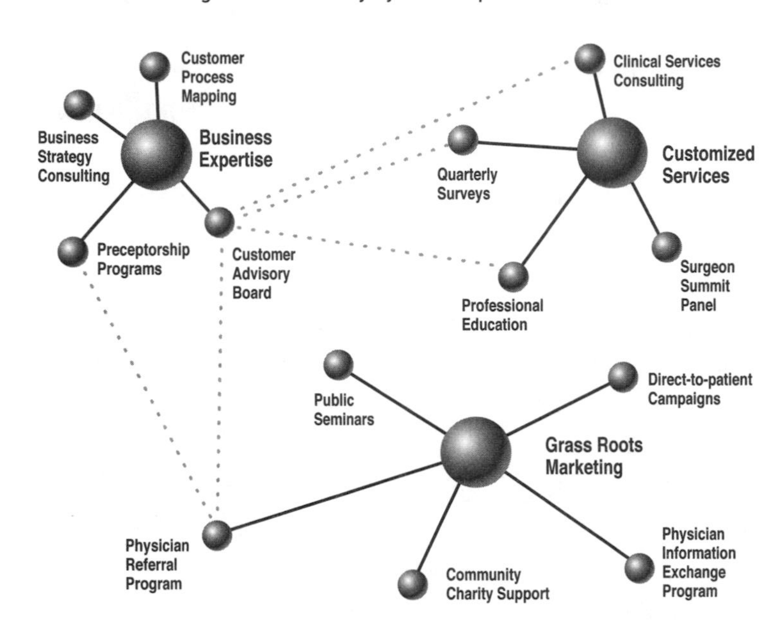

4. Rate tactics around each strategic theme, relative to one another on their level of impact (Low—Medium—High).
5. Consider eliminating tactics that have a low impact.

After creating the Activity System Map, ask these questions:

1. Do the strategic themes collectively embody a strategy differentiated from the competition?
2. Is each tactic supporting at least one strategic theme?
3. What is the overall level of tactical value (connectivity + impact)?
4. Is each tactic directly or indirectly relevant to customers?
5. Sketch a key competitor's Activity System Map. What insights can you draw from comparing your Activity System Map to theirs?

When it comes to action, this Norwegian proverb serves as a good reminder: "The hungriest wolves hunt best." Complacency, recent success, and a lack of urgency are all potentially dangerous undertows to effective strategy execution. Being alert to the five execution errors, becoming reacquainted with the definitions of business planning terms, and applying tools such as the Stategy-Print, Strategy Formula, and Activity System Map all provide a solid start in tackling the discipline of action's considerable challenge. Unless we work for Sun Tzu, there's no sense losing our heads over execution.

PEARLS OF INSIGHT

- **Managers make five common errors in executing strategy:**
    1. Faulty strategy
    2. Unclear resource requirements
    3. Poor communication
    4. Weak accountability
    5. Lack of calibration
- **The Resource Allocation Calculator is a tool for evaluating whether or not a strategy has sufficient resources for successful implementation.**
- **The StrategyPrint is a two-page business blueprint that serves as a real-time strategic action plan for a business.**
- **The Strategy Tune-up is a periodic (e.g., weekly, monthly, quarterly) meeting with key personnel for strategy development and execution to review context of the business.**
- **Remember to use G.O.S.T. terms correctly, and not interchangeably.**
    - Goal: A general target—What, *generally*, you are trying to achieve.
    - Objective: Specific outcome desired—What, *specifically*, you are trying to achieve.

- Strategy: The resource allocation plan—How, *generally*, to achieve the goals.
- Tactic: The tangible activities/items that carry out the strategies—How, *specifically*, to achieve the goals.

○ **Strategy Formula = WHAT + HOW + WHO + IMPACT**

- WHAT: The activity representing the purpose of the strategy.
- HOW: The general means or method of accomplishing the strategy.
- WHO: The audience the strategy is designed to reach.
- IMPACT: The desired result of developing and executing the strategy.

○ **The Activity System Map is a visual representation of an organization's strategy and the tactics that support it. It provides a thirty-thousand-foot view of the business by capturing the strategy and tactics, and relationships between the two, on a single page.**

CHAPTER 6

TEAM DIVING

The mind, that ocean where each kind
Does straight its own resemblance find;
Yet it creates, transcending these,
Far other worlds and other seas.

—Andrew Marvell, poet

The process of helping managers develop their strategic thinking skills enables an organization to become more competent overall in strategy development and execution. Jeanne Liedtka, executive director of the Darden School's Batten Institute, writes: "A premium is now placed on producing a high quality of 'strategic thinking' at all levels in the organization, and on the skill set to manage conflict productively. Thus, building a widely distributed strategy-making process requires strategic thinking at the individual level as well as the ability to use this as input into a larger conversation whose outcome is coherent at the organizational level."[1]

By embedding the three disciplines of strategic thinking—acumen, allocation, and action—at the individual level, an organization can create a core competency that continually fuels competitive advantage. Vivien Cox, chief executive for Gas, Power, and Renewables at BP, says: "As people at all levels become more sophisticated and strategic in their outlook, strategy can move from an individual capability to an institutional capability. And with that transition, the quality and speed of our business improves as it increasingly reflects knowledge and insights from across the hierarchy."[2]

Academic research has confirmed the economic value of superior strategic thinking skills to the organizational level. The Evergreen Project out of Harvard University is the most statistically rigorous management research ever conducted on the keys to enduring business success. The study examined more than two hundred management practices, from innovation and business processes to 360-degree performance reviews. A total of 160 companies were reviewed over a ten-year period to determine which of the management practices were essential to a company's financial success. The financial measurements included total return to shareholders, sales, assets, operating income, and return on invested capital. Strategy development and strategy execution were two of only four management practices out of two hundred found in every single financially successful company. No exceptions. The firms with strong strategy development and strategy execution outperformed the losing companies by a 945 percent to 62 percent margin in total return to shareholders; a 415 percent to 83 percent advantage in sales; a 358 percent to 97 percent advantage in assets; a 326 percent to 22 percent advantage in operating income; and a 5.45 percent to -8.52 percent advantage in return on invested capital.[3]

By embedding the three disciplines of strategic thinking—acumen, allocation, and action—at the individual level, an organization can create a core competency that continually fuels competitive advantage.

World-class organizations understand the urgency in providing training and tools for their managers to become more effective strategists. For example, GE places great importance on having managers who are skilled at strategic thinking, as evidenced in the article "GE's Next Workout . . . Teach Every Manager to Be a Strategist." Bob Corcoran, former director of Crotonville, was quoted in that article as saying, "Jeff [Immelt, CEO of GE] inherited a company skilled at execution—one that can stop on a dime and deliver results. The company just loves to execute. Now the question is how to develop the top line."[4]

It appears the answer to that question about growing the top line resides in the minds of GE's managers: "The purpose is to systematically build the capabilities of managers throughout the company—capabilities that enhance strategic thinking and cut down on bureaucratic decision making. In other words, GE wants smart managers to be able to make the kind of strategic judgments and bets on bold new projects that would have been made by only the most senior executives in the past."[5]

Art Kleiner, editor of *Strategy + Business,* which published that article, writes, "If you bring smart people together regularly to step back from the day-to-day urgencies and improve their work, with a clear line of accountability for results afterward, it's amazing what can happen."[6] Strategic thinking is that mental "step back," providing a forum for individuals and teams to reflect on the business and continually generate insight.

While the benefits of developing individual and organizational competency in strategic thinking are becoming more familiar to senior leaders, significant barriers to building a broad-based strategic-thinking capability still exist. In a study of fifteen large companies in twelve industries, the following eight barriers were identified, and they are listed in order of prominence.[7]

1. Focus on short-term objectives (80 percent)

2. No common language or process for strategy (73 percent)
3. Lack of strategy skills in managers (66 percent)
4. Culture not supporting fact-based debate (66 percent)
5. Minimal resources committed to strategy (53 percent)
6. Hierarchical decision making (53 percent)
7. Capability building not a high priority (47 percent)
8. Lack of accountability for strategy (33 percent)

A common element exists among the eight barriers—lack of a clear and compelling long-term purpose.

DISCOVERING PURPOSE—MISSION, VISION, AND VALUES

That business purpose and business mission are so rarely given adequate thought is perhaps the most important cause of business frustration and failure.

—Peter Drucker, management guru

Why did you attend that meeting this morning? Why have you chosen to pursue customer segment X and not customer segment Z? The answers should support your business purpose, either current or future. Understanding *why* is perhaps the most motivating and success-driving reason for realizing your full potential. As a French researcher once noted, "Those who know why they are fighting will win over those who don't."

Purpose comes in three forms: (1) current purpose, or mission; (2) future purpose, or vision; and (3) guiding purpose, or values. A **mission** is a clear, concise, and enduring statement of the reasons for an organization's existence today. A **vision** represents future purpose, providing a mental picture of the aspirations an organization is working toward. Supporting both the current and the future purpose are values. **Values** are the ideals and principles that guide the thoughts and actions of an organization and define its character. Working together (as represented in Figure 6.1), mission, vision, and values provide a powerful directional force for unifying and coordinating actions and decisions to ensure the optimal use of resources.

Because strategy is concerned with the intelligent allocation of limited resources, identifying a current and future purpose is critical. Strategically speaking, establishing a clear and compelling purpose provides the general basis or criteria that resource allocation decisions should be made on and measured against. Without

Figure 6.1 Purpose

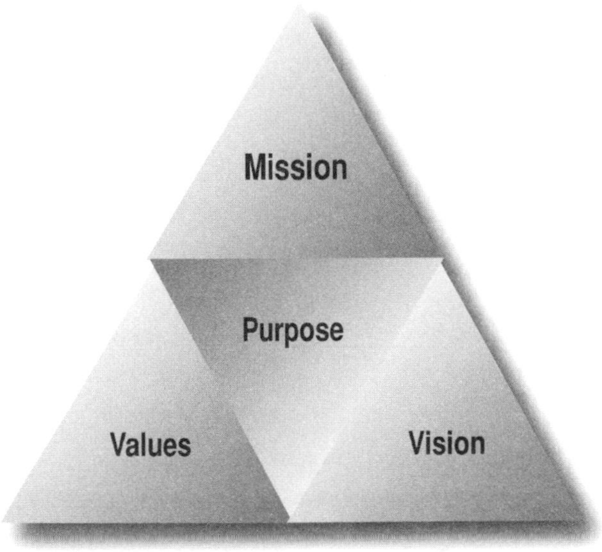

Mission
Purpose
Values
Vision

purpose, the rationale for decision making becomes subjective and disconnected from the company's goals and objectives.

Current Purpose: Mission Statement

A mission is the current reason for being. Why is this organization in business? What is the marketing group's purpose? How does an individual manager contribute to the overall cause? Although a seemingly simple proposition, creating an effective mission statement can be one of the most challenging aspects of strategic thinking because it forces examination to answer the question, *why*? It is also one of the most overlooked parts of strategy development; everyone just assumes they are working toward the same purpose. However, the perils of this assumption cannot be underestimated.

> Because strategy is concerned with the intelligent allocation of limited resources, identifying a current and future purpose is critical. Without purpose, the rationale for decision making becomes subjective and disconnected from the company's goals and objectives.

As human beings, we are driven to a great extent by our emotions. In order to take advantage of the power of the organization's emotional energy, rationale born from this emotion is necessary to complement the financial and business reasons for work. While the paycheck is important, it provides only one side of the "why we're here" coin. Creating a sound current purpose addresses the other side of the coin. To generate the greatest creativity and extricate the deepest level of talent from an organization, don't tell them what to do and how to do it—tell them who they are. Defining the mission, vision, and values accomplishes that task.

The mission statement also frames the business strategy. Since the scope of business, customer targets, and competitive arena are addressed in the mission statement, it naturally defines the business strategy. It also forces decisions of what not to do, one of the key characteristics of strategic thinking. It is in this process of choosing what not to do and who not to target as customers that the business focus emerges. The importance of focus was clearly articulated by the noted military historian B.H. Liddell Hart when he said, "The principles of war can be condensed into one word—concentration."[8]

One element of the mission often overlooked is the importance of the belief and commitment to it once it is developed. As with the U.S. Constitution and the Bible, a mission statement is effective strictly for those who believe in it. The belief must go hand in hand with the commitment to follow it. A New Year's resolution is worthless in and of itself. It is the commitment to the resolution that matters, as evidenced by all the resolutions that have gone by the wayside.

Once the organization's mission is in place, mission statements for departments and functional groups within the organization may be helpful. Mission statements at these levels tend to be more specific, and they more closely reflect the daily activities of the particular group. Developing these sub-mission statements also clarifies the "why" at that level and creates greater team unity—both of which make for a stronger organization.

Benefits of a Mission Statement

The mission statement gives everyone a baseline that guides and unifies strategic choice. Without a current purpose, or mission, you won't have an objective basis against which to measure the decisions you make.

Second, the mission statement ensures that different functional groups within the organization and individuals within departments have the same rationale for their actions. Acting as a compass, the mission ensures that everyone is pulling in the same direction.

Third, the mission statement addresses the deeper, emotional component of why people do what they do for an organization or customer base. In other words, it taps into the right brain (emotional, intuitive, visual, and synthesizing). The left brain (logical, reasoning, quantitative, analyzing) is satisfied by the intellectual rigor of the work and the paycheck; the right brain needs something more, something that appeals to the emotional side. The mission statement thus fulfills that emotional need, creating a satisfied whole.

Fourth, research has shown that companies with a well-crafted mission statement have greater financial success and are recognized for superior quality as compared to companies with poor or nonexistent mission statements.[9] Other studies have reported firms working according to a mission statement have a 30 percent higher return on certain financial measures than firms without mission statements.[10] Identifying and articulating a mission statement not only makes common sense but also makes financial sense.

Finally, the current purpose, or mission statement, acts as a rallying point for people in good times and in bad times. A mission statement focuses people on the truly important things that will drive success. In difficult times, the mission statement is a reminder to stay on the task at hand. It also helps prevent people from becoming reactive to minor competitor moves and keeps them focused on the course that has been set.

Mission Statement Criteria

One way to ensure that a mission statement is fulfilling its potential is to rate it according to five criteria. Score one point for each of the following questions, with a perfect score being five points:

1. What function is performed?
2. How is it performed?
3. For whom is it performed?
4. Why is it performed?
5. Does the tone convey the company's uniqueness?

What function is performed? The first question to be answered is, "What do you do?" On the surface, this may seem ridiculously obvious. Give it some thought. In his landmark article "Marketing Myopia," Harvard professor Theodore Levitt challenged people to step back and think about their functions in a more expansive way. He argued that one of the reasons the railroad industry met with a dramatic decline is they viewed their function as moving things by rail, when they could have defined their function more inclusively as transportation. This may have freed their minds to adapt to the changing business landscape and re-create their offering to remain a more relevant fixture in the marketplace.[11]

How is the function performed? Strategy is based on competition. When considering this second question in formulating a mission statement, assess how the competition performs the function. Then ask, "Are we performing the function in a unique manner? If not, how long will we last before this lack of differentiation reduces our offering to a commodity?"

For whom is the function performed? Who is benefiting from the function? More important, who is paying for the value generated by the function? The customer group identified in the mission statement should be focused enough to allow concentration of sales and marketing resources, but broad enough to provide a sustainable source of revenue. Perhaps the single biggest sales and marketing error of trying to be "all things to all people" usually occurs because companies haven't defined their market properly during the development of the mission statement.

This question also helps define market segments and market fragments. Market segments are groups that are divided up by the marketer based on the marketer's designated criteria. The most common segmentation criteria are the details of demographic information (i.e., geography, age, income level, budget, etc.).

Market fragments, on the other hand, are initially formed by the customers, not by the marketers. This occurs when a group of customers fragments, or breaks off, from a traditional segment to pursue something different. For example, when beer drinkers started turning their tastes toward the handful of microbrew beers, the mass beer producers took notice of this trend, or market fragmentation, and capitalized on it by creating their own microbrew beers.

Why is the function performed? One of the characteristics of a good mission statement is that it captures the motivation of why you do what you do. It tugs at the emotional, or right-brain, component in each of us and gives that raison d'être that keeps people interested in meeting the daily challenges to reach their goals. It also places "the job" in a larger community context and gives people a more meaningful purpose for their efforts.

The answers to these four questions form the basis of the mission statement. In developing responses, be specific enough to create focus, but likewise be broad enough to allow for flexibility in the day-to-day execution. When the mission statement begins to come together, it is also important to ensure that it represents the uniqueness of the organization. The litmus test is to replace your company's name with a competitor's name in the mission statement. If it works with the competitor's name, you haven't captured the unique characteristics of your organization, and you need to rework it.

Tone

After creating the first draft, begin to hone the words so the language and tone reflect the culture of the organization. A perfect example is the renowned Johnson & Johnson company credo. The credo represents the family quality of the company through its language and tone: "We believe our first responsibility is to the doctors, nurses and patients, to mothers and fathers and all others who use our products and services . . ."[12]

Infusing a mission statement with the tone of the organization's values and culture helps further brand the company's current purpose in the hearts and minds of employees and customers. By using language that works on both the logical and the emotional level, the mission statement motivates employees to put forth their best efforts to contribute to the overall good of the organization.

If your mission statement didn't score at least four points, it would be worthwhile to rethink it and determine what's missing.

Examples of Mission Statements

The following verbatim examples of mission statements provide a look at the variety of ways to convey your business's current purpose. Notice the distinct tone that represents the essence of each company. Following each mission statement is its score based on the five criteria.

LEGO

> The purpose and vision of the LEGO Group is to inspire children to explore and challenge their own creative potentials.
>
> - We strive to accomplish this by offering a range of high-quality and fun products centered around our building systems.
> - In the hands of children, the products inspire the unique form of LEGO play that is fun, creative, engaging, challenging—all at the same time.
> - This activity supports the child, giving it the special pride of accomplishment. In the process it "automatically" or playfully develops a set of future, highly relevant capabilities: creative and structured problem

> solving, curiosity and imagination, interpersonal skills, and physical motor skills—building with LEGO bricks is thus about "learning through play."

Score = 5 points

Comments: LEGO thoroughly covers each of the five areas, and their uniqueness shows through because the statement would not fit their competitors.

Lexus Covenant

- Lexus will enter the most competitive, prestigious automobile race in the world.
- Over fifty years of Toyota automotive experience has culminated in the creation of Lexus cars.
- They will be the finest cars ever built.
- Lexus will win the race because Lexus will do it right from the start.
- Lexus will have the finest dealer network in the industry.
- Lexus will treat each customer as we would a guest in our home.
- If you think you can't, you won't . . .
- If you think you can, you will!
- We can, we will.

Score = 4 points

Comments: The "Covenant" is a strong variation of a mission statement that admirably represents its uniqueness in the market. More specificity on "whom they serve" would enhance it.

Cirque du Soleil

> Cirque du Soleil is an international company from Quebec dedicated to the creation, production, and distribution of artistic works. Our mission is to invoke the imagination,

> provoke the senses and evoke the emotions of people throughout the world. *Cirque du Soleil* is a generator of new experiences, a laboratory and platform for creators. We are constantly researching new artistic avenues and innovating within our organization—and we intend to carry on taking such risks and inventing with audacity.
>
> As we pursue our dreams and grow our business it is also our intention to position ourselves in the community as an agent of change. We will, as a matter of policy, treat our employees, clients, partners, and neighbors with respect, and willingly operate our business according to the laws of every jurisdiction we work in. In all our relationships—internal and external—we will always go the extra mile as proof of our daring and creativity.

Score = 5 points

Comments: An excellent mission statement that captures the essence of the organization, which can be challenging when creating new market space. The attitude of Cirque is evident throughout and adds to the representation of their uniqueness.

In summary, a good mission statement meets the following criteria: is clear; answers What? How? Who? and Why?; captures uniqueness; reflects values; and is motivational.

Future Purpose: Vision Statement

The future purpose of the organization is described through a vision statement, creating a mental picture of what the purpose will look like in the future. While the mission statement answers What is the purpose today? the vision statement answers Where is our purpose headed in the future? Being able to answer the questions, Where are we today? and Where are we going? is a vital combination for the strategist.

DIVE MASTER PRACTICE

Review your business mission statement and see if it addresses the following five questions. For each question it addresses, score one point.

1. What function is performed?
2. How is it performed?
3. For whom is it performed?
4. Why is it performed?
5. Does the tone convey the company's uniqueness?

How many points did your mission statement score out of possible five points? Which areas of the mission statement can be enhanced to create a more meaningful mission?

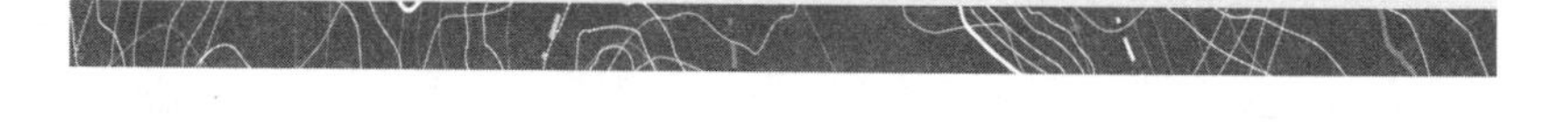

The vision statement provides two things: strategic guidance and motivational focus. The strategic thinking that goes into creating the vision statement ensures that it represents the best use of the organization's resources in reaching its objectives. The vision statement serves to align individuals from different functional areas and geographic locations to move toward the same future purpose, allowing them to use their creativity and talents to get from "here to there." It guides actions not necessarily geared toward the short term by showing the desired longer-term future and the benefits of realizing that future.

The vision statement provides two things: strategic guidance and motivational focus.

Similar to the mission statement in that it utilizes the emotional, or right-brain, energy of individuals, the vision statement also encourages motivation. This differs from the motivation encouraged in the mission statement in that it focuses on aspiration, or that which is yet to be realized. Whereas the mission statement represents the purpose being lived out today, the vision statement represents the purpose as a goal still to be achieved. Robert Greenleaf, in his groundbreaking work *Servant Leadership*, defines vision as "The overarching purpose, the big dream, the overarching concept . . . something presently out of reach . . . so stated that it excites the imagination and challenges people to work for something they do not yet know how to do."[13]

Criteria for a Vision Statement

In his work *Leading Change*, professor John Kotter of the Harvard Business School outlines six characteristics of a sound vision statement,[14] which I've paraphrased in the following list:

1. Imaginable: It needs to paint a visual picture of the desired future in the minds of those who read it.
2. Desirable: It should appeal to the people who are striving to reach it and the customers they are serving.
3. Feasible: While aspirational in nature, it needs to articulate a realistic and achievable future purpose.
4. Focused: It should provide concentrated direction to those following it.
5. Flexible: By being broad in scope, it allows for modifications due to the dynamic nature of the business environment.
6. Communicable: The vision statement should be easy to articulate to others.

Capturing the essence of these six characteristics in the vision statement often requires considerable thought and time. Review your organization's vision statement. How well does it address each of the six criteria? Rate your vision by giving it one point for each of the six criteria. If it doesn't score at least four points, it would be worthwhile to rework it.

Examples of Vision Statements

Vision statements are generally more concise than mission statements, and in some cases they are short enough to put on a bumper sticker. They also tend to play to the grand scheme of things, bringing together the feasible and the incredible. Here are some notable verbatim examples.

Avon

> Our vision is to be the company that best understands and satisfies the product, service and self-fulfillment needs of women globally. Our dedication to supporting women touches not only beauty—but health, fitness, self-empowerment and financial independence.

Comments: A strong and succinct statement that could benefit from a slightly more aspirational component.

Hertz

> We will be the first choice brand for vehicle and equipment rental/leasing and total mobility solutions.

Comments: Clear and concise with a definite focus. Lacking in the imagination and desirability areas.

The Coca-Cola Company

> To achieve sustainable growth, we have established a Vision with clear goals:
>
> - People: Being a great place to work where people are inspired to be the best they can be.
> - Planet: Being a responsible global citizen that makes a difference.

- Portfolio: Bringing to the world a portfolio of beverage brands that anticipate and satisfy people's desires and needs.
- Partners: Nurturing a winning network of partners and building mutual loyalty.
- Profit: Maximizing return to shareowners while being mindful of our overall responsibilities.

Comments: A thorough vision that encompasses all key internal and external groups. Profit is not usually a good candidate for inclusion in vision statements, however, as quantification tends to be less aspirational from an emotional perspective.

In summary, a good vision statement meets the following criteria: creates a mental picture of future purpose; is a strategic guide; is imaginable, desirable, feasible, focused, flexible, and communicable.

Guiding Purpose, or Values

Engrained in the current and future purpose are values—the ideals and principles that guide the thoughts and behavior of an organization. Because values represent the core beliefs, they are a powerful shaper of an organization's culture. Values shape the conduct of people in their interactions with customers, suppliers, vendors, and each other. They also provide another benchmark in the daily decision-making process. The chosen course of action must comply with the values in order to be considered a good decision.

Although individuals possess different types of values, there are several reasons why organizational values *should not* be produced by company-wide consensus. First, there are probably a number of employees who don't belong at the company, and their input may not accurately represent the best interest of the whole. Second, it assumes all input is equally valuable, which may not be the case.

Therefore, the most trusted members of the group—usually the founder(s)—should identify the core values.

In order to have their full effect, values should be integrated into all aspects of the company, from the interview and candidate-selection process to setting the criteria for employee dismissal. Once again, we see the powerful emotion-driven, or right-brain, component at work; it is engaged by values and acts as a strong complement to the logical "right and wrong" reasoning of individuals. As with purpose, the strength and effect of values depend on how deeply they are believed and the ensuing commitment to them.

As with purpose, the strength and effect of values depend on how deeply they are believed and the ensuing commitment to them.

One of the common mistakes in identifying values is to list terms that are honorable and worthy but are not held in deep belief by the organization. For instance, it is difficult (if not impossible) to value both "highest quality" and "frugality," even though they may both be desirable. It is also helpful to list those values that give the organization its unique character. If the company has a number of stories of how its employees have gone the extra mile in providing top-quality customer service, it would be fair to list "service" as a value. However, if the company's customer service is just average, listing it as a value weakens the overall perception because it's not a deeply embedded belief.

Examples of Values

Here are a few examples of companies and their respective values reproduced verbatim. As you'll notice, they each restrict their list to between three to five values. A laundry list of more than five becomes unwieldy in the day-to-day decision-making process.

Adidas

- We are consumer focused and therefore we continuously improve the quality, look, feel, and image of our products and our organizational structures to match and exceed consumer expectations and to provide them with the highest value.
- We are innovation and design leaders who seek to help athletes of all skill levels achieve peak performance with every product we bring to market.
- We are a global organization that is socially and environmentally responsible, creative, and financially rewarding for our employees and shareholders.
- We are committed to continuously strengthening our brands and products to improve our competitive position.
- We are dedicated to consistently delivering outstanding financial results.

Whole Foods

- Selling the Highest Quality Natural and Organic Products Available
- Satisfying and Delighting Our Customers
- Supporting Team Member Excellence and Happiness
- Creating Wealth Through Profits and Growth
- Caring About Our Communities and Our Environment

Four Seasons Hotels and Resorts

Building Communities: Four Seasons is committed to being a responsible and caring community partner, by having a positive economic impact and supporting community goals, both within and outside the hotel. We engage in innovative training and mentoring programs for young people; support those in need; and celebrate the diverse cultures where Four Seasons operates.

Advancing Cancer Research: Four Seasons is committed to supporting both local efforts and broader campaigns whose goal is the eradication of cancer. Through the collective efforts of the company's hotels worldwide, Four Seasons annually raises significant funds and awareness for cancer research.

Supporting Sustainability: Four Seasons involves employees and guests in the common goal of preserving and protecting the planet. We engage in sustainable practices that conserve natural resources and reduce environmental impact. As importantly, sustainable tourism will enhance and protect the destinations where Four Seasons operates for generations to come.

In each of the previous examples, the values provide guidelines for how employees should behave with respect to their customers, their colleagues, and their communities. A good set of values meets the following criteria: it represents ideals and principles; it guides action and decision making; it provides foundation for mission and vision; and it is true to the organization.

THE STRATEGY DEVELOPMENT PROCESS

An organization's purpose in the form of mission, vision, and value statements is an important component of the strategy development process. While this book has provided a road map for individuals to enhance their strategic thinking skills, it is understood that creating forums for team strategic thinking as part of an overall strategy development process is essential. The following section will cover five phases of the strategy development process (see Figure 6.2) and discuss the key aspects of each.

Figure 6.2 Strategy Development Process

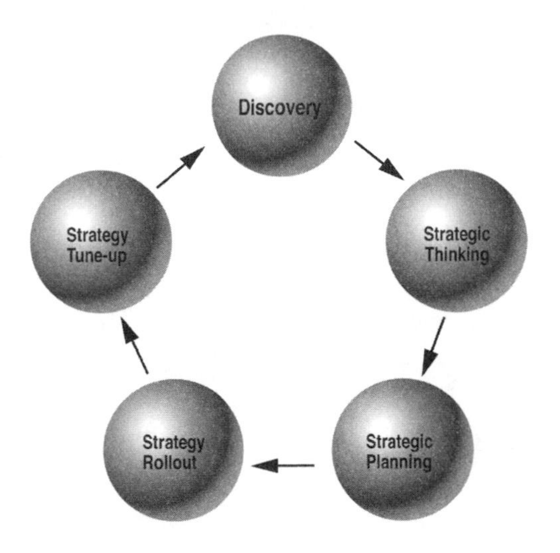

The process of developing strategy is similar to the process divers use to create their adventures. Both require the vision to see the finished form, and the skill, insight, and courage to create it. Therefore, we describe the five phases of the best-of-breed strategy development process, in concert with the five phases of diving.[15]

I. Discovery: "Research the Dive"

Divers begin by researching dive sites, selecting their crew, and compiling information on what they will be viewing underwater. Similarly, the discovery phase of strategy development involves selecting the people, process, and information to be used.

The discovery phase entails the designation of the strategy development team, an outline of the process being used, and pre-work. The pre-work involves intelligence gathering on the market, customers, competitors, and the company, including primary research with customers and employees in the form of one-to-one interviews or focus groups.

In addition to this information, the strategy development team members should complete a Strategy Survey that focuses their thinking on the critical areas of the business and begins preparing them for the strategic thinking sessions. It is important to have team members fill out the Strategy Survey individually. Research has shown that brainstorming individually *prior* to group discussion is always more productive in both the quality and the quantity of thinking than group brainstorming. The Strategy Survey I've designed contains five sections of questions: Market, Customers, Competitors, Company, and Strategy. The sample excerpts from the Strategy Survey that appear in the following box will help you get a better idea of the types of questions to ask.

The Strategy Survey stimulates the team's thinking prior to the group strategy sessions and thereby makes those sessions more productive. Be sure to include the Strategy Survey in your strategy development process to "prime the pump" and begin capturing the insights that will fuel your plan. (See sample questions from the Strategy Survey on pages 160–161.)

II. Strategic Thinking: "Envision the Dive"

Once divers have selected the dive site, chosen the crew, and researched the underwater sites, they begin to mentally map out the different aspects of the dive. In every detail—from type of equipment to coral formations and cave explorations to day-versus-night dives—divers mentally envision what the dive will look like. The strategic thinking phase provides the forum to begin generating and capturing business insights around the four key areas of the business: market, customers, competitors, and the company.

The most common reason why organizations turn out strategic plans that don't move the needle is the belief that strategic thinking and planning are the same thing. Strategic thinking is the generation of insights about a business, while strategic planning takes those insights and transforms them into an action plan to achieve the company's goals and objectives. Strategy development without the "thinking" phase is akin to an organizational lobotomy. The models introduced earlier in this book are examples of the types of tools used from a pool of more than forty to facilitate team strategic thinking. The selection of the appropriate models is a key element in the successful application of team strategic thinking to the strategy development process.

III. Strategic Planning: "Plan the Dive"

Our divers are now ready to board the ship and head out to the dive site. On the way to the site, they plan the dive with their diving buddy and the dive master. They discuss how long they will be underwater, where they will go, what signals to use in case of emergency, etc. The strategic planning phase acts in the same manner, creating the framework for the strategy and all its elements. It transforms the insights generated from strategic thinking into the strategic action plan that achieves the organization's goals and objectives and includes the appropriate time lines and budgets. The deliverable from the strategic planning phase is the StrategyPrint—the two-page blueprint for the business that was discussed in the section on strategy execution.

IV. Strategy Rollout: "Perform the Dive"

Our divers are now ready to take their dive. After entering the water, they check their equipment and gauges and proceed below the surface. In the same way, the strategy rollout phase transforms the strategic plan into activities and offerings that move the business forward. This phase ensures that the key elements of the strategic action plan are clearly communicated throughout the organization and that an implementation plan is in place.

The first step is to create an implementation plan that provides the direction and the details of how the strategic plan will be executed. What follows is a checklist of the key areas to address in designing a solid implementation plan (continues on page 162).

Sample of the Strategy Survey

Market

- What is the current state of the market? (check one and complete rate)

  Growing ☐ Stable ☐ Declining ☐ Rate: ___%

- What is the market structure? (check one box for each)

Barriers to entry	Low ☐	Medium ☐	High ☐
Power of customers	Low ☐	Medium ☐	High ☐
Power of suppliers	Low ☐	Medium ☐	High ☐
Threat of substitutes	Low ☐	Medium ☐	High ☐
Industry competition	Low ☐	Medium ☐	High ☐

Customers

- How do you add value to the customer?
- List the top three customer value drivers and rate your company versus your best competitor on scale of 1–10, with 1 being low ability to meet value and 10 being high ability to meet value.

Primary customer group: ______________________________

Customer Value Drivers	My Score	My Best Competitor's Score
1. ________________	______	______
2. ________________	______	______
3. ________________	______	______

Competitors

- Who are your closest competitors? Why?
- Name your top three competitors and the three points of differentiation for each from your customer's perspective.

Competitor	Points of Differentiation
1. ______	1. ______
	2. ______
	3. ______
2. ______	1. ______
	2. ______
	3. ______
3. ______	1. ______
	2. ______
	3. ______

Company

- What is the organization's purpose?
- What are the organization's core competencies?

Strategy

- What criteria are used for resource allocation?
- What is the company's profit model (how do you make money)?
- How do you communicate strategy throughout the organization?

☑ **Purpose**—What purposes is the plan designed to achieve? Are they clearly articulated in the form of vision, goals, and objectives?

☑ **Resources**—What are the resources (tangible, intangible, and human) that will be allocated to achieve the plan's purposes?

☑ **Accountability**—Which individuals and functional groups are responsible for achieving each of the goals?

☑ **Time Frame**—What are the time parameters associated with the elements of the plan?

☑ **Budget**—How much will each item identified in the plan cost to implement?

☑ **Alignment**—Are all of the functional groups (marketing, sales, project management, IT, etc.) aligned to achieve the same goals, or will groups be pulling in different directions?

☑ **Metrics**—Are clear, consistent, and realistic metrics in place to monitor progress?

☑ **Project Template**—Is a singular project template in place to ensure that all projects consuming resources are meeting the agreed-upon strategic criteria?

☑ **Communication Tools**—Have the appropriate communication vehicles been identified to convey key information of the strategic plan to all employees?

Once the implementation plan has been developed and resource levels have been assessed, there are five steps (as depicted in Figure 6.3) to follow to facilitate a smooth strategy rollout.

The following steps support the strategy rollout:

1. Development of the communication plan.
2. Dissemination of the strategic action plan to employees through the chosen communication vehicles.

Figure 6.3 Strategy Rollout

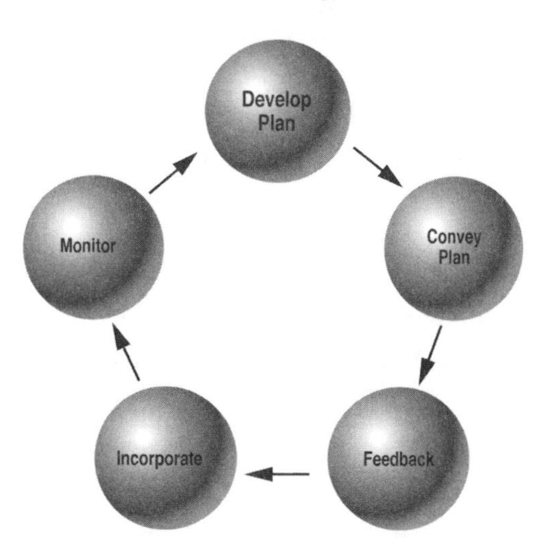

3. Collection and review of feedback regarding the strategic action plan components and the effectiveness of their communication to the organization.
4. Incorporation and application of the strategic action plan to employees' daily activities and their corresponding metrics.
5. Periodic pulse-taking to monitor progress and assess effectiveness and relevance of both the strategy and the tactics, as well as employees' understanding of each.

V. Strategy Tune-up: "Review the Dive"

Once the divers complete their dive and return to the boat, they record and review the key elements of the dive including depth, bottom time, visibility, etc. Similarly, the strategy tune-up phase serves to keep the strategy evergreen.

Constituting a half-day to one-day session every quarter, the strategy tune-up consists of formal reviews of the business by the strategy development team to hone their work. The team methodically reviews the four key areas of the business to identify changes and make any necessary adjustments to strategy and tactics.

LEADING A STRATEGY WORKSHOP

A thoughtfully crafted and professionally facilitated strategy workshop is a key component of the strategy development process. Strategy workshops provide a forum for formal conversations about a group's strategic direction. J. Bruce Harreld, senior vice president of marketing for IBM, shares the importance of a strategy workshop for his organization: "The essence of strategy is disciplined, fact-based conversations. This approach now involves more than 25,000 general managers at IBM in both the formulation and execution of strategy."[16]

A strategy workshop provides the following benefits:

- Creates a shared understanding of the business. By having a thorough discussion around the four key areas of the business (market, customers, competitors, and the company), you can ensure that people in different functional areas and at different levels are all working in the same direction.
- Generates innovation. True strategic thinking requires you to challenge your assumptions about the business. When you challenge even the most basic of assumptions, you begin generating new insights, which lead to new value for customers—the basis of innovation.
- Creates prepared minds. Strategy workshops serve the dual purpose of developing strategy and training your managers on the key concepts, tools, and frameworks of strategy. Strategy workshops can develop managers' strategic thinking skills in a practical and interactive way.

- Evaluation of managers' business acumen. It is one thing to be good at filling out a PowerPoint template on planning. There is a potential world of difference in being able to contribute to a live discussion on strategy. This requires the ability to effectively listen to others (which few can or choose to do), synthesize facts from different areas, and generate new business insights in a real-time setting. As a senior leader, there is no better forum in which to evaluate the strategic capabilities of your managers.

Creating the Strategy Workshop

There are five steps to running a solid strategy workshop.

1. Determine the intent of the workshop. What are the goals for the workshop? Is it part of an overall strategy development process? How does it fit into the business?
2. Identify the participants. Is there representation from all key functional areas? Is the meeting limited to only senior executives, or does it include highly strategic middle managers as well? Research has shown that more than half (56 percent) of strategy workshops don't include any middle managers, potentially excluding the views of those closer to customers.[17] Not including managers responsible for overseeing the strategy's implementation can inadvertently create a barrier, as author Fiona Czerniawska reports: "When asked about the single most significant obstacle to implementing strategy, [the] most common response was that people lacked a sense of ownership of the strategy and therefore did not feel responsible for its successful implementation."[18]
3. Provide a pre-workshop Strategy Survey. In order to maximize time during the workshop, it is critical to have participants think through and capture relevant business intelligence beforehand. A tool such as the Strategy Survey

provides a brief but comprehensive guide for managers to use as they consider what the most important pieces of the business are. Research has shown that 45 percent of workshop participants spend less than half a day preparing before the session.[19] This lack of preparation prior to the workshop drains valuable face-to-face meeting time and is a result of poor planning.

4. Prepare and focus the group with pre-reading. Providing the group with one or two reasonable reading assignments (articles, book chapters, etc.) before the workshop educates the team on important concepts, tools, and frameworks. Pre-reading also focuses the team on the strategic perspective necessary for the workshop, helping them elevate their thinking beyond the day-to-day tactical operations that can choke big-picture insights.
5. Design the meeting framework. As a senior leader, your reputation is on the line when you put together a strategy workshop. Nothing can destroy a team faster than a meeting with a vague agenda, rambling off-point discussions, and a weak facilitator. A good facilitator has expertise in the strategy process; can identify the handful of models (out of the potential forty or so) that are right for each specific team and their business; and can skillfully lead the group through the complex and nonlinear path of strategic thinking. Regarding facilitation, Gerard Hodgkinson, professor at Leeds University Business School, says, "It may be beneficial to employ external facilitators to neutralize political pressures and conflicts and to prevent an over-reliance on such experience-based knowledge which otherwise might limit the range of strategic issues discussed and the perspectives considered."[20]

After the initial strategy workshop, a list of action steps, responsibility, and accountability should be developed along with a time line. A follow-up workshop should be conducted approximately four weeks later to report on the progress made since the team was last together. It is also important to agree on a tool the group will use to capture key insights from the strategy workshop. This tool will act to highlight key business intelligence collected in the selected repository vehicle (intranet pages, database, etc.) on an ongoing basis.

Properly done, the strategy workshop provides an effective and efficient means for educating, inspiring, and preparing your management team to excel in their business. Improperly done, the strategy workshop wastes time, eats away at morale, and creates doubt in a team's mind about the competency of their leader.

PEARLS OF INSIGHT

- **Purpose comes in three forms: current purpose (mission); future purpose (vision); and guiding purpose (values).**
- **A Mission is a clear, concise, and enduring statement of the reasons for an organization's existence today.**
- **A Vision represents future purpose, providing a mental picture of the aspirational existence that an organization is working toward.**
- **Values are the ideals and principles that guide the thoughts and actions of an organization and define its character.**
- **The strategy development process has five phases:**
    1. Discovery—"Research the Dive"
    2. Strategic Thinking—"Envision the Dive"
    3. Strategic Planning—"Plan the Dive"
    4. Strategy Rollout—"Perform the Dive"
    5. Strategy Tune-up—"Review the Dive"
- **The four main benefits of a well-designed strategy workshop are:**
    1. It creates a shared understanding of the business.
    2. It generates innovation.
    3. It creates prepared minds.

4. It is a vehicle to evaluate a manager's business acumen.

- **The five steps to preparing a successful strategy workshop include:**
    1. Determine the intent of the workshop.
    2. Identify the participants.
    3. Provide a pre-workshop Strategy Survey.
    4. Prepare and focus the group with pre-reading.
    5. Design the meeting framework.

CHAPTER 7

DEEP DIVE DANGERS

> A smooth sea never made a skillful mariner, neither do uninterrupted prosperity and success qualify for usefulness and happiness. The storms of adversity, like those of the ocean, rouse the faculties, and excite the invention, prudence, skill and fortitude of the voyager.
>
> **—Thomas L. Haines, author**

Even the best-intentioned strategists are occasionally caught up in the undertow of flawed strategic thinking.

Our human nature predisposes us to a number of biases that, left unchecked, can severely hamper our best intentions when it comes to thinking and acting in a strategic manner. Developing an awareness and understanding of these potential barriers can ensure that we're making important decisions and strategic trade-offs to the best of our abilities. This chapter discusses the nine Deep Dive Dangers to be aware of as you apply strategic thinking on a daily basis. For each of the deep dive dangers, a life preserver of three techniques is provided to save you from falling victim to these insidious flaws in strategic thinking.

1. ABSOLUTE PERFORMANCE

One popular myth in many organizations is "as long as we do what we do best, we don't have to worry about what the competition is doing." Wrong. In business, never forget that your performance is relative, not absolute. Just because you're producing the best products you've ever produced and your customer service ratings are as high as they've ever been, you are not guaranteed success. As Phil Rosenzweig, professor at IMD, has pointed out, while GM was producing the best cars they've ever produced and Kmart was continually improving its inventory management, procurement, and automated reordering, both fell further behind in their markets.[1] This was because their competition had mastered those areas to a greater degree, as GM's market share continued to slide and Kmart was forced into bankruptcy.

While we don't want to emulate what competitors are doing, we must have a clear understanding of what they are doing and how it is perceived by customers relative to our offerings. Robert Rubin, former U.S. Treasury Secretary and Goldman Sachs executive, says: "Once you've internalized the concept that you can't prove anything in absolute terms, life becomes all the more about odds, chances, and trade-offs. In a world without provable truths, the only way to refine the probabilities that remain is through greater knowledge and understanding."[2]

Life Preserver: To avoid the danger of absolute performance in strategic thinking, consider the following:

- Measure your progress against other organizations.
- Create a system to monitor and record business intelligence (market, customers, competitors, and the company) and make it available to managers.
- When internal factors such as sales force or R&D are declared strengths, ask how they stack up against the best in the industry.

2. ANCHORS

In making decisions, the mind tends to give initial information or impressions a disproportionate amount of weight. This tendency is referred to as an "anchor." The anchor jades the decision-making process because it starts the process at an artificially high or low point. Numerous studies have shown that when an anchor is used at the beginning of the process, people do not sufficiently adjust from that initial anchor value to a more accurate one.

A study of real estate appraisers and the effects of anchoring showed that by changing only one piece of information (the listing price) in a ten-page package of materials, the researchers were able to shift the real estate appraisal by more than $10,000.[3] Anchors are intentionally used in nearly all types of negotiations to sway the process in favor of the party using the anchor. Examples of anchors include a low base salary on a job offer, last year's budget, and a customer's artificially low price request.

Anchors can affect strategic thinking in a similar way. Most commonly, anchors take the form of last year's strategic plan or this year's financial forecast. By using the assumptions that went into last year's plan, strategy becomes fatally flawed. Strategic thinking demands that all assumptions, beliefs, and information be looked at from a fresh perspective on a continual basis. Simply tweaking last year's plan is a major disservice to your business because it suffocates any chance of discovering new insights that may dramatically alter the strategic direction.

The bureaucracy in many companies dictates the development of budgets prior to the development of strategy. This is a real challenge for large and small businesses alike. Unfortunately, budget numbers anchor people's thinking in a minimalist approach, as the nature of budgeting requires. Budgets and forecasts can create a faulty anchor by stifling strategic thinking with "the numbers" instead of a thorough review of the business.

Allowing the budget anchor to initiate the strategy development process is like tying down the wings of an eagle and saying, "I know your wings are tied down, but I still need you to circle that mountaintop. Are you with me? You can do it. Remember the motto this year is 'Whatever it takes!'" Sound familiar?

Strategic thinking demands that all assumptions, beliefs, and information be looked at from a fresh perspective on a continual basis.

Life Preserver: To avoid the danger of anchors in strategic thinking, consider the following:

- Create an open mind by actively considering the range of starting points available, not just the anchor point.
- View the issue from different frames (e.g., marketing manager should seek views of HR, sales, and operations managers).
- Identify anchors as soon as they appear and call them out mentally and physically (on paper/PC/flip chart) so everyone is aware of their presence.

3. BENCHMARKING

On the surface, benchmarking gives the appearance of one of those activities that unquestionably add value to an organization. And therein lies its danger. When benchmarking best practices, it is critical to understand what exactly is being benchmarked. The first discipline of strategic thinking is acumen, and a key aspect of successfully generating insight is to understand the context. The context of best practices includes such things as culture, compensation, market state, competitive position, leverage relative to suppliers, customer influence, etc. A thorough understanding of the entire system of strategy supporting best practices is critical. Equally important are the relationships (both manifest and latent) among the key elements of the system. A less-than-complete understanding of the context, system, and relationships can cause one to miss the essential components that lead to successful application of best practices.

Professor Jeffrey Pfeffer of Stanford's Graduate School of Business playfully points out: "Southwest Airlines is the most successful airline in the history of the industry. Herb Kelleher, its CEO from 1982 to 2001, drinks a lot of Wild Turkey bourbon. Does this mean that your company will dominate its industry if your CEO drinks a lot of Wild Turkey?"[4]

Life Preserver: To avoid the danger of benchmarking in strategic thinking, consider the following:

- Identify what exactly is being benchmarked.
- Describe the context in which the benchmarked practice is occurring and compare it to your situation.
- Identify the strategy ecosystem of the benchmarked practice and the relationships involved in the system.

4. CONFIRMATION BIAS

Computers have the ability to analyze in a completely objective manner. Human beings do not. Subconsciously, people tend to make decisions first and look for information afterward to support their decisions. Confirmation bias is the human condition of seeking data and information to support what you believe while discounting evidence to the contrary. This condition causes intelligent people to ignore facts that clearly point in an opposite direction. A prime example of this was provided by a former CEO of Polaroid in an interview just prior to their filing Chapter 11: "Before we start, let me premise that there is one thing about photography that not everyone understands but that is crucial to it. In the photography business all the money is in the software, in the consumables. There is no money in the hardware. This has always been and will always be a fundamental truth."[5]

Good strategists understand that they bring a particular frame to viewing their business. Becoming locked into that frame causes people to dismiss other frames and perspectives without giving them proper consideration.

Another aspect of not using available information comes from the fact that if you are not looking for something, then it usually goes unnoticed. Anyone who travels by air is accustomed to the security "obstacle course" that must be traversed. Researchers from Harvard Medical School and Brigham and Women's Hospital re-created the weapons-screening process used in airports. Here is an account of their findings: "Study participants screened bags for dangerous objects after having been told how often those objects would appear. When they were told that the objects would appear 50 percent of the time, participants had just a 7 percent error rate. But when they were told that the objects would appear only 1 percent of the time, the error rate jumped to 30 percent."[6]

In this example, the fact that people weren't expecting to see objects actually caused them to stop actively looking for them. In business, not being prepared to look for new insights, changes in the market, and shifts in the competitive landscape can quickly derail strategic initiatives.

Life Preserver: To avoid the danger of the confirmation bias in strategic thinking, consider the following:

- Record the evidence for each position in a ledger format to enhance an objective view.
- Acknowledge the underpinnings of your reason for taking a position and consider the opposite motivations.

- Bring in someone to present the other positions to provide a fresh perspective.

5. FORECASTING

> In business, not being prepared to accept new insights, changes in the market, and shifts in the competitive landscape can quickly derail strategic initiatives.

The mere act of attempting to estimate or calculate something in advance should give you pause: amateurs—in some cases monkeys—routinely outperform experts in meteorology and the stock market. There are several traps to be aware of when forecasting in business. The first is overconfidence. As human beings, we're prone to overestimating our talents, which you could argue is also the reason some people succeed in overwhelmingly difficult conditions. A study of one million students by the College Board in the 1970s asked them to rate themselves versus their peers on several measures. For leadership ability, 70 percent rated themselves above average, while only 2 percent rated themselves below average. For athletic ability, 60 percent rated themselves above the median, and only 6 percent rated themselves below average.[7]

A second trap of forecasting involves recollection. Recollection involves placing undue emphasis on more dramatic events or data because they tend to stick in your mind. For example, this phenomenon causes people to overestimate the total number of shark attacks each year because they receive a disproportionate amount of attention in the media. The data reveal that the chance of being killed by a shark is actually thirty times less than dying from falling airplane parts.[8] In an organization, a high-profile risk taken to produce an innovative product that fails will weigh much more heavily in a manager's mind than will a lower-profile success of the same financial magnitude.

A final trap of forecasting involves the use of averages. It has become a shortcut in many aspects of business to use averages as a convenient way of arriving at an answer more quickly. The good strategist realizes that while averages can be appropriate in some situations, they can be fatal in others. Author Sam Savage provides a clever example: "Consider the case of the statistician who drowns while fording a river that he calculates is, on average, three feet deep. If he were alive to tell the tale, he would expound on the 'flaw of averages,' which states, simply, that plans based on assumptions about average conditions usually go wrong."[9]

Life Preserver: To avoid the danger of forecasting in strategic thinking, consider the following:

- Overconfidence: Use a range with the extremes as bookends to estimate a spectrum of values.
- Recollection: Identify the data or facts for the events to ground your thinking in an objective base.
- Averages: Use a range of numbers whenever possible versus a single figure.

6. GROUPTHINK

Strategic thinking and strategic planning are often done in a group setting. Consequently, it is important to recognize the influence of groupthink. Groupthink occurs when there is a homogenous group of people with little influence from outside sources and a high level of pressure to conformity.[10] Groupthink tends to directly and indirectly reduce the level of objective thinking, remove devil's-advocate thinking, and punish those who attempt to do either.

Irving Janis, a former research psychologist at Yale University, describes eight symptoms of groupthink,[11] which I've paraphrased in the list that follows. As you participate in your group's next strategic thinking or planning session, try to observe if any of these symptoms are present:

1. Illusion of invulnerability that leads to over-optimism and excessive risk-taking
2. Efforts to rationalize or discount warning signs
3. No challenges to collective thinking
4. Stereotyped views of competitors as inconsequential
5. Pressure on group members who disagree with the majority
6. Shared illusion of unanimity
7. Self-correction when thinking of diverting from group consensus
8. Information sought only to support group consensus; unwillingness to look for or consider information that is contrarian (also known as the "confirming evidence bias")

Another reason to consider using an external resource to facilitate strategy workshops is that groupthink occurs quite commonly. A third party can effectively neutralize the effects of groupthink by providing an outsider's perspective and objectively challenging participant responses. Just as surgeons don't operate on themselves or family members because of the procedural and emotional difficulty, businesses should get a second opinion when it comes to their strategic thinking.

Life Preserver: To avoid the danger of groupthink in strategic thinking, consider the following:

- Assign one person in the group to play devil's advocate and take the opposite position of the majority.
- Utilize an external resource to ensure objectivity and divergent opinions.

- Bring in people from other functional areas (marketing, R&D, IT, HR) to offer fresh perspectives.

7. HALO EFFECT

The halo effect is the habit of making specific conclusions based on a general overall impression. First articulated by psychologist Edward Thorndike and recently applied to business management by professor Phil Rosenzweig, the halo effect describes how people tend to take a company's positive or negative performance and apply it to the specific elements of the business without a direct correlation of cause. Rosenzweig shows how popular business books such as *In Search of Excellence, Built to Last,* and *Good to Great* all suffer from the halo effect.[12] In each book, the authors use data contaminated by the halo effect to show cause of performance (e.g., high performance because of certain traits) when in fact they are merely representing attributions or results of performance.[13] In general, the books say that a few elite companies outperformed their competitors *because* of certain traits. However, since the data sources were not independent of performance (e.g., glowing reviews in magazine and newspaper articles), the claim of traits as a direct cause of performance cannot be validated.

The halo effect can cause managers to try to emulate the components of a successful company (structure, leadership, strategy, innovation, etc.) without realizing those components may not have had a significant contribution to that organization's success. Sound strategic thinking requires managers to not mindlessly follow a flavor-of-the-month formula for success.

The halo effect also manifests itself in managers applying techniques that were successful for them in the past to future situations, even though the circumstances may be dramatically different. As noted earlier, a thorough understanding of the specific context is required before any reasonable course of action can be taken. Unfortunately, the popular formulaic business books usually fail to take context into account, which dramatically diminishes their value.

Life Preserver: To avoid danger of the halo effect in strategic thinking, consider the following:

- Carefully assess the sources of data being used to understand their level of bias.
- Visually diagram the system involved to help identify causes, effects, attributions and unintended consequences.
- Understand the context in which the event or issue is unfolding prior to suggesting actions. Recall the three disciplines of strategic thinking: acumen, allocation, and action.

8. STATUS QUO

Popular adages such as "If it ain't broke, don't fix it," "Don't rock the boat," and "Let sleeping dogs lie" all feed into the natural tendency to prefer the status quo. Time and again, research has proven that when individuals have the option of doing something new or staying with the status quo, they overwhelmingly stay with the status quo.

Feeding into the danger of always leaning toward the status quo is the fact that human beings are generally risk averse. Since departing from the status quo opens you up to risk—and, with risk, potential failure—it is easy to understand why people are content with the status quo. Unfortunately, in some cases the status quo is the least desirable option and will potentially lead to decline.

Research in the field of decision making by Amos Tversky and Daniel Kahneman has shown that preferences between gains are risk averse and preferences between losses are risk seeking.[14] Risk aversion occurs when a certain outcome is preferred to a gamble with an equal or greater (monetary) expectation. If the gamble with equal expectation is preferred, it is risk seeking. Tversky and Kahneman cite the following example:

> Imagine you are forced to choose between two options: Option 1 is a sure gain of $80. Option 2 offers an 85 percent chance of winning $100 and a 15 percent chance of winning nothing. Most people choose option 1, the certain gain, as opposed to the gamble, despite the fact that the gamble has a higher monetary expectation than the certain outcome. The following analysis of the options shows the true probabilities:
>
> Option 1: $80 × 1 (certain) = $80 average monetary gain
>
> Option 2: $100 × .85 (probability) + $0 × .15 (probability) = $85 average monetary gain
>
> So, despite the fact that option 2 will, on average, provide a better monetary gain, people are psychologically predisposed to risk aversion when facing a loss and will select option 1.[15]

In general, the threat of a loss has a greater effect on a decision than the possibility of an equivalent gain. The response to loss is more extreme than the response to gain.

Consequently, many strategy decisions place too much weight on the potential negative outcomes because, psychologically, the displeasure associated with losing a sum of money or market share points is greater than the pleasure associated with gaining the same amount. This principle

> The response to loss is more extreme than the response to gain. This principle of human nature has a strong effect on strategy decisions and must be taken into account to avoid always acting in a risk-averse manner when the probability of success is actually greater.

of human nature has a strong effect on strategy decisions and must be taken into account to avoid always acting in a risk-averse manner when the probability of success is actually greater.

Life Preserver: To avoid the danger of the status quo in strategic thinking, consider the following:

- Focus on the outcome desired and use that as a measurement between the status quo and other alternatives.
- Examine the actual changes that would need to be made to abandon the status quo, as the reality is often less painful then imagined.
- Explore a range of alternatives outside the status quo to provide a full picture of the potential courses of action and their accompanying benefits.

9. SUNK-COST EFFECT

People who have played a hand of poker know the difficult decision of folding their cards (dropping out of the game) when they have invested a considerable amount of money in the pot. The flawed rationale is: "Well, I might as well stay in the game because I've already put a lot of my chips into the pot. What's the harm of putting in a few more chips now?" This tendency affects managers in the high-stakes game of resource allocation as well, and it is known as the sunk-cost effect.

Sunk costs are previous investments that are no longer recoverable. Research has indicated a bias toward making a choice that justifies a previous decision, even when that decision no longer appears to be valid.[16] On the surface, it seems ludicrous that a manager would continue to invest new resources in an initiative that is clearly not working. Nevertheless, managers are often unwilling to admit a mistake, and shutting down an initiative opens that manager up to review and potential criticism. Consequently, if managers work in a culture where mistakes are directly or indirectly punished, they may very well fall into the sunk-cost effect because the other option of pulling the plug and admitting even a temporary defeat is not tenable.

Life Preserver: To avoid danger of the sunk-cost effect in strategic thinking, consider the following:

- Use the blank-slate test: starting from today, what is the best use of resources moving forward, with no consideration given to past decisions?
- Ask someone detached from the situation to provide thoughts on the current decision and the best option moving forward.
- Determine the type of culture and environment in which decisions are made. Is it conducive to admitting mistakes

DIVE MASTER PRACTICE

Write down the nine deep dive dangers on a 3 x 5 note card. Bring the note card with you to all your meetings for the next week. After each meeting, place a check mark next to the type of flawed strategic thinking that occurred during the meeting. At the end of the week, total the number of times each deep dive danger occurred. Which type of flawed strategic thinking is most common in your organization? What steps can you and your team take to prevent these deep dive dangers from sinking future meetings?

and moving on, or does it motivate people to "stay the course at all costs" and foster the sunk-cost effect?

While we can't always ensure the successful outcomes to strategic decisions, we can greatly improve our process for arriving at those decisions. Developing an awareness and understanding of the nine Deep Dive Dangers will go a long way in helping our business fend off the competitive sharks and successfully navigate the sometimes murky waters of strategic thinking.

PEARLS OF INSIGHT

- **There are nine Deep Dive Dangers managers need to be aware of when it comes to strategic thinking.**
  1. Absolute Performance: forgetting that performance is always relative to the competition.
  2. Anchors: giving initial information or impressions a disproportionate amount of weight.
  3. Benchmarking: taking an incomplete view of what exactly is at the root of another firm's success.
  4. Confirmation Bias: seeking out data and information to support what one believes while discounting evidence to the contrary.
  5. Forecasting: being overconfident, giving prominence to what is first recalled, and using an average when a range of numbers would be more precise.
  6. Groupthink: the effect of a homogenous group of people with little influence from outside sources and a high level of pressure to conform.
  7. Halo Effect: the habit of making specific conclusions based on a general overall impression.
  8. Status quo: a person's preference for continuing with the same, instead of trying something new.
  9. Sunk-Cost Effect: a bias toward making a choice that justifies a previous decision, even when that decision no longer appears valid.

CHAPTER 8

THE CONFIDENCE TO DIVE

> I was like a boy playing on the seashore and diverting myself now and then finding a smoother pebble or a prettier shell than ordinary, whilst the great ocean of truth lay all undiscovered before me.
>
> **—Isaac Newton, physicist, mathematician, and astronomer**

The term *design* is normally used to describe the endeavors of those who work in such areas as architecture, engineering, and fashion. Rarely are the words *strategy* and *design* used in the same sentence, much less in the same concept. Yet, the definition of design—"the purposeful or inventive arrangement of parts"—describes exactly what a manager does when thinking strategically.[1] Good strategists are continually moving the puzzle pieces of the business system around in their mind to create the advantage they need to succeed. Adding to the degree of difficulty is the fact that the puzzle pieces are constantly changing shapes and sizes. Customer value drivers change, competitors introduce new products, and market dynamics shift, all of which cause the business system to act more like the broken pieces of colored glass in a kaleidoscope than the view from a clear window.

STRATEGY DESIGN

The Strategy Design is a tool to help managers make sense of their kaleidoscope of business (see Figure 8.1). It is a culmination of strategic thinking concepts and tools that acts as the lighthouse for those doing deep dives. The Strategy Design provides managers with the bearings they need to continually keep their businesses on course, despite the waves of meaningless activities and tactics crashing in all around them. It comprises the seven salient aspects of the strategic direction for a business, whether the business is an entrepreneur or a Fortune 500 multinational corporation.

The seven components of the Strategy Design are briefly described in the paragraphs that follow.

Purpose

The purpose is the reason your company exists in the marketplace. It answers the deeper question of why you do what you do. Purpose can take the form of mission (current purpose), vision (future purpose), and values (guiding purpose). Identifying a clear purpose will pave the way for stronger decision making because it provides clear criteria for the type of actions and offerings that should guide your company.

Figure 8.1 Strategy Design

Purpose	Reason
Value	Type
Context	Situation
Who	Customer
What	Offering
How	Capabilities
Advantage	Differentiation

Value

Research has shown that when companies focus a disproportionate amount of their resources on one of the three value disciplines (product leadership, customer intimacy, or operational excellence), they have greater financial success than their peers who do not.[2] When managers choose the primary type of value they will offer customers—best product, best cost, or best solution—they are able to use this focus as a guide for both internal (colleagues, employees) and external (customers, shareholders) partners.

Context

The context is a description of the current situation. It provides a snapshot of what the environment, opportunities, and threats might be. In many circles, the context is referred to as the situation analysis. The appropriate actions can be taken only when the context is clear. Without a keen understanding of the situation, it is impossible to intelligently allocate resources and select strategic initiatives because their success hinges on relative, not absolute, performance.

Who

Selecting the customer group to serve and the customer groups not to serve are critical factors in setting strategy. Although it is common to take business from any customer that comes in off the street, it is certainly not practical or profitable to do so. Ensuring that managers and differing functional units within an organization are targeting the same customer type greatly leverages the efforts of individuals into a collective whole. Selecting which customer to serve can often be a make-or-break decision that seldom receives the attention it deserves. The question, Which potential customers are we choosing not to serve? provides a starting point for the conversation.

What

Asking what your company is offering may seem a bit rudimentary, like asking fish what they do in the water. In some cases, the answer might be that simple. In many organizations, however, there are numerous offerings, each of which provides a drastically different return on investment. Taking time to define the offering—its components, services, etc.—will provide a strong foundation when you are assigned the task of comparing your offerings to competitors' or collecting customer feedback. Defining your company's offerings also sheds light on the depth of thinking. Does a bus company offer passenger travel or transportation solutions? The answer can lead you down very different paths.

How

In the earlier section on competitive advantage, it was suggested that competitive advantage begins with an organization's capabilities. Capabilities consist of the resources and core competencies that fuel the activities that lead to offerings. "How" asks what the distinct capabilities the company possesses are in order to create value for customers. Capabilities may include intellectual property, specific technologies, functional expertise, brand architecture, and others. The key is to understand what drives the creation of your company's offerings.

Advantage

At the end of the day, all hard work must result in an advantage. The ability to produce positive differentiation that yields superior value to customers separates the best from the rest. Managers who operate with a Beach Bum mentality will always lag behind Free Divers, that is, those who are willing to take the risk of free diving to produce deep insights. Differentiation that customers value is the driving force behind an organization's success.

Figure 8.2 Strategy Design—CustoSolution

Purpose	Provide surgeons with the best combination of product & service
Value	Customer intimacy–best total solution
Context	Old technology not tailored to surgeons' new techniques
Who	General surgeons at academic hospitals
What	CustoSolution medical device
How	Product development by thought-leading surgeons
Advantage	Medical device wrapped in business & clinical consulting services

Now that we understand the seven components of the Strategy Design, let's apply them. For example, the Strategy Design for the fictitious medical device company CustoSolution might look like that illustrated in Figure 8.2.

In the dark storms of activity that can cloud your judgment, the Strategy Design serves as a lighthouse, continually reminding you of your strategic direction. Meanwhile, the challenge of competition and reaching your full potential calls you back to the sea to engage in your daily business battles.

APPLYING THE THREE DISCIPLINES

Former world chess champion Garry Kasparov reminds us that having the tools alone to think strategically is not enough: "Finally, we come to the hardest part of developing and employing strategic thinking: the confidence to use it and the ability to stick to it consistently. Once you have your strategy down on paper, the real work begins. How do you stay on track, and how do you know when you have slipped off away from thinking strategically?"[3]

There is an ocean of concepts, tools, and frameworks to guide strategic thinking, and therein may lie the greatest challenge. This

DIVE MASTER PRACTICE

Using the seven elements, create the Strategy Design for your business. Are any of the seven elements not completely clear or certain? Review the Strategy Design with several colleagues. Do they view the individual elements of the Strategy Design in the same way you do? Review the Strategy Design with members of different functional areas. Do they all have the same vision of the Strategy Design as you do? If not, where are the variances?

book was written to help managers at all levels successfully navigate the uncharted waters of their minds and build tangible skill sets in strategic thinking. The three disciplines of strategic thinking offer a simple yet comprehensive way to apply strategic thinking to your daily business.

Dozens of principles and models have been discussed for each discipline to provide an array of methods for applying strategic thinking to business. While the sheer number of those principles and models can at first appear to be overwhelming, the three-A's framework—acumen, allocation, and action—will continually guide you toward their proper application. Based on the disciplines, there are three questions managers can use daily to stimulate strategic

Figure 8.3 Strategic Thinking Discipline Questions

Discipline	Question
Acumen	What is the key insight?
Allocation	Where will I focus resources?
Action	How will I achieve advantage?

thinking and ensure that they are periodically doing their deep dives (see Figure 8.3).

> The three disciplines of strategic thinking—acumen, allocation, and action—offer a simple yet comprehensive way to apply strategic thinking to your daily business.

These three questions can help managers continually assess their businesses from a strategic perspective. Strategy begins with acumen, and acumen demands that we work to generate insight. Too often business amounts to nothing more than a flurry of tactics that are reactions to everything from off-base customer requests to minor changes in competitor advertising. The first discipline of strategic thinking reminds us to continually ask the question, What is the key insight?

Allocation of resources resides at the heart of strategy. Allocation sets the wheel of strategy in motion by directing resources to specific areas and activities. This direction of resources must clearly designate the "nots"—the areas that are not receiving resources as well as those that are receiving resources. Strategy is as much about what you choose *not* to do as it is about what you choose *to* do.

Finally, the discipline of action focuses attention on the end game of strategic thinking—competitive advantage. The concept of strategy originally sprang from the military arena and the need for one group to defeat another. A subtle difference between thinking in general and strategic thinking in particular is that strategic thinking always seeks to gain an advantage. Once a manager has developed insight and allocated resources, the final task is to shape those resources into activities that will lead to advantage. The question, How will I achieve advantage? provides the lighthouse toward which you must continually swim, no matter how strong the opposing tide of commodity status pulls at you.

Mastering the techniques of the three disciplines of strategic thinking enables us to do our daily deep dives, searching for those pearls of insight that lead to competitive advantage. With the vision of "pearls of insight" fresh in our minds, let's close with a story.

Back in 1870, free divers collected precious milky-white gems known as pearls. On a single breath, they would dive below the water's surface, sometimes to depths of a hundred feet, and search for oysters that contained these prize pearls. One summer, as the legend goes, two boys were living in a small seaside village: one age seventeen and one age ten. Each day, the boys would head to the ocean and free dive in search of oysters that held pearls. As the sun began to dip in the late afternoon, they would return to the village with their burlap sacks filled with oysters. The older boy would dump his oysters on the large wooden table of the village elder and talk for hours of his adventures. Meanwhile, the younger boy, who normally collected only a few small oysters, would sit quietly off to the side.

"Why don't you tell them about your oysters?" chided the older boy. But the younger boy just sat silently, staring off toward the sea.

Then one day, something strange happened. When the two boys returned that afternoon, the village elder asked the older boy, "How were your dives today?" Without a word, the older boy opened his sack above the table and turned it over. Nothing came out—not a single oyster.

The village elder turned to the younger boy and asked, "How were your dives today?" The young boy struggled to lift his sack over the table and then turned it over. Out fell dozens of the largest oysters the villagers had ever seen. Not believing his eyes, the older boy stammered, "But where did you find these oysters? We dive in the same waters."

"Yes, it is true that we dive in the same waters. Only today, I dove thirty feet deeper than you to find these pearls," said the young boy.

"But how were you able to dive deeper than me? After all, I have more experience than you," replied the older boy.

The younger boy said, "It is simple. Each afternoon, as you talked hour after hour about your experience, I sat silently . . . and practiced holding my breath."

To realize our full potential, to maximize our chances of success, and to outperform our competition, we need to think strategically. Remembering the three disciplines of strategic thinking, we need to continually sharpen our "acumen," intelligently "allocate" our resources, and "act" on the important things in our lives. As the English poet Robert Browning reminds us:

> There are two moments in a diver's life.
> One, when a beggar, he prepares to plunge,
> Then, when a prince, he rises with his prize.

PEARLS OF INSIGHT

- **The Strategy Design is a culmination of strategic thinking concepts and tools that provide managers with the bearings they need to keep their business on course. It consists of the seven salient aspects of the strategic direction for a business:**
  1. Purpose—the reason you exist in the marketplace
  2. Value—the primary type of value you provide (best product, best cost, best solution)
  3. Context—the description of the current situation
  4. Who—the customer group you are targeting
  5. What—the offering you are providing to customers
  6. How—the distinct capabilities the company possesses to create value for customers
  7. Advantage—the differentiated value you provide to customers

- **Ask these three questions to apply the three disciplines of strategic thinking on a daily basis:**
  1. Acumen—What is the key insight?
  2. Allocation—Where will I focus resources?
  3. Action—How will I achieve advantage?

NOTES

Chapter 1

1. Jay Jamrog et al., "Leading into the Future: A Global Study of Leadership 2005–2015," *American Management Association* (2006).
2. Bill Torbert, *Action Inquiry* (San Francisco: Berrett-Koehler, 2004).
3. B. Garratt, *Developing Strategic Thought: Rediscovering the Art of Direction-Giving* (London: McGraw-Hill, 1995).
4. Robert Kaplan and David Norton, "The Office of Strategy Management," *Harvard Business Review* (October 2005).
5. Heike Bruch, "Beware the Busy Manager," *Harvard Business Review* (February 2002).
6. Michael Mankins, "Stop Wasting Valuable Time," *Harvard Business Review* (September 2004).
7. Ingrid Bonn, "Developing Strategic Thinking as a Core Competency," *Management Decision* 39 (2001).
8. Matthew Olson, Derek van Bever, and Seth Verry, "When Growth Stalls," *Harvard Business Review* (March 2008).
9. Michael Porter, excerpt, *European Strategy Program* brochure.
10. Brian Tracy, *Executive Excellence,* vol.14 (December 1997).
11. Clayton Christensen, "Making Strategy: Learning by Doing," *Harvard Business Review* (November–December 1997).
12. Arlene Mayzel, "Techies Need to Know the Business," *BW Chicago* (March 2008).
13. Noel Tichy and Warren Bennis, *Judgment* (New York: Portfolio, 2007).

14. J. E. Hunter and R. F. Hunter, "Validity of Common Methods for Predicting Job Success," *Psychological Bulletin* (1984).
15. Arlene Weintraub, "The Lawyer Is In at Pfizer," *Business Week* (August 14, 2006).
16. David Mayer and Herbert Greenberg, "What Makes a Good Salesman," *Harvard Business Review* (July–August 2006).
17. Matthias Hild and Tim Laseter, "Reinhard Selten: The Thought Leader Interview," *Strategy + Business* (Summer 2005).
18. William Pagonis, "Leadership in a Combat Zone," *Harvard Business Review* (December 2001).
19. Dan Lovallo and Lenny Mendonca, "Strategy's Strategist: An Interview with Richard Rumelt," *The McKinsey Quarterly* (August 2007).
20. Henry Mitzberg, "The Rise and Fall of Strategic Planning," *Harvard Business Review* (January–February 1994).

Chapter 2

1. Bruce Horovitz, "CFO Anderson to Lead Wendy's," *USA Today* (April 18, 2006).
2. Sandra Jones, "Macy's Reaching Out to Lure Former Field's Shoppers," *Chicago Tribune* (December 13, 2006).
3. Scott Hensley, "As Generics Pummel Its Drugs, Pfizer Faces Uncertain Future," *Wall Street Journal* (January 2006).
4. Doug Ross, "A New View of Strategic Leadership," *Strategy Magazine* (March 2007).
5. Gerrard Hodgkinson et al., "The Role of Strategy Workshops in Strategy Development Processes," *Long Range Planning* 39 (2006).
6. Rich Horwath, *Sculpting Air: The Executive's Guide to Shaping Strategy* (Illinois: SC, 2006).
7. Margaret Peteraf (chapter author), Joseph Bower, and Clark Gilbert, *From Resource Allocation to Strategy* (New York: Oxford University Press, 2005).
8. Bruce Henderson, "The Origin of Strategy," *Harvard Business Review* (November–December 1989).
9. Jeffrey Immelt, "Letter to Stakeholders," *GE 2003 Annual Report* (February 13, 2004).

10. Michael Raynor, "Solving the Strategy Paradox: How to Reach for the Fruit Without Going Out on a Limb," *Strategy & Leadership* 35, no.4 (2007).
11. *The American Heritage Dictionary of the English Language*, 4th ed. (Boston: Houghton Mifflin Company, 2000).
12. David Besanko et al., *Economics of Strategy*, 3rd ed. (New Jersey: John Wiley & Sons, 2004).
13. Michael Porter, "The Five Competitive Forces That Shape Strategy," *Harvard Business Review* (January 2008).
14. Margaret Peteraf, "Competitor Identification and Competitor Analysis," *Managerial and Decision Economics* 23, no. 4–5 (June–August 2002).
15. Clayton Christensen et al., "Innovation Killers: How Financial Tools Destroy Your Capacity to Do New Things," *Harvard Business Review* (January 2008).
16. James Allen, "Diamond in the Rough," *Business Strategy Review* (Autumn 2007).
17. Stephen Tallman in David Faulkner and Andrew Campbell, eds., *The Oxford Handbook of Strategy* (New York: Oxford University Press, 2003).
18. Ibid.
19. Kevin Coyne, "Sustainable Competitive Advantage," *The McKinsey Quarterly* (November 1984).
20. Bruce Chew, "The Geometry of Competition," *Monitor Group* (2000).
21. Michael Treacy and Fred Wiersema, *The Discipline of Market Leaders* (New York: Perseus Books, 1995).

Chapter 3

1. Roger Martin, "How Successful Leaders Think," *Harvard Business Review* (June 2007).
2. John Forsyth, "Capitalizing on Customer Insights," *The McKinsey Quarterly*, no. 3 (2006).
3. Tim Laseter and Rob Cross, "The Craft of Connection," *Strategy + Business* (Autumn 2006).
4. Gordon Shaw, "Strategic Stories: How 3M Is Rewriting Business Planning," *Harvard Business Review* (May–June 1998).

5. James Hackett, "Sustaining the Dream," *Business Week* (October 15, 2007).
6. Robert Kaplan and David Norton, "The Office of Strategy Management," *Harvard Business Review* (October 2005).
7. Editor-in-Chief, "Thinking about Thinking," *Technology Review* (February 2004).
8. Jia Lynn Yang, "He's at the Head of the Class," *Fortune* (February 19, 2007).
9. David Rock and Jeffrey Schwartz, "The Neuroscience of Leadership," *Strategy + Business* (Summer 2006).
10. Ibid.
11. Tribune News Services, "Dell Net Falls 18%; Sales Fight Cited," *Chicago Tribune* (May 19, 2006).
12. Anthony Mayo and Nitin Nohria, "Zeitgeist Leadership," *Harvard Business Review* (October 2005).
13. Phil Vettel, "Le Francais Swallowed Up by the Competition It Inspired," *Chicago Tribune* (June 8, 2007).
14. Peter Johnson, "Couric: I Went to CBS with Eyes 'Wide Open,'" *USA Today* (May 10, 2007).
15. Theodore Levitt, "What Business Are You In," *Harvard Business Review* (October 2006).
16. *The American Heritage Dictionary of the English Language*, 4th ed. (Boston: Houghton Mifflin Company, 2000).
17. Jeffrey Immelt, "Letter to Stakeholders," *GE 2003 Annual Report*, February 13, 2004.
18. Quinn Spitzer and Ron Evans, *Heads, You Win!* (New York: Fireside, 1999).
19. Gerrard Hodgkinson et al., "The Role of Strategy Workshops in Strategy Development Processes," *Long Range Planning* 39 (2006).
20. Niccolo Machiavelli, *The Prince* (New York: Random House, 1908).
21. Henry Mintzberg, "The Strategy Concept: The Five P's of Strategy," *California Management Review* 30, no. 1 (1987).
22. Robert Pitkethly in David Faulkner and Andrew Campbell, eds., *The Oxford Handbook of Strategy* (New York: Oxford University Press, 2003).

23. Clayton Christensen, "Beyond the Innovator's Dilemma," *Strategy & Innovation* (March–April 2003).
24. J. Randel, H. Pugh, and S. Reed, "Methods for Analyzing Cognitive Skills for a Technical Task," *International Journal of Human-Computer Studies* (1996): 579–97.
25. Keith Hammonds, "The Strategy of the Fighter Pilot," *Fast Company* (June 2002).
26. Pitkethly, in Faulkner and Campbell, *Oxford Handbook.*
27. Kevin Coyne, "Breakthrough Thinking from Inside the Box," *Harvard Business Review* (December 2007).
28. Michel Robert, *Strategy Pure and Simple II* (New York: McGraw Hill, 1998).
29. Ken Demma et al., "The New Learning Curve," *Marketing Management* (July–August 2005).
30. Steve Hamm, "The Vacuum Man Takes on Wet Hands," *Business Week* (July 2, 2007).
31. Tim Laseter, "See for Yourself," *Strategy + Business* (Autumn 2007).
32. Joseph Bower, Clayton Christensen and Clark Gilbert, *From Resource Allocation to Strategy* (New York: Oxford University Press, 2005).
33. Jamie Dimon, "Building the Global Bank: An Interview with Jamie Dimon," *The McKinsey Quarterly*, no. 4 (2006).
34. Mihaly Csikszentmihalyi, *Creativity* (New York: HarperPerennial, 1996).
35. James Young, *A Technique for Producing Ideas* (Illinois: NTC Business Books, 1975).
36. David Myers, "The Powers and Perils of Intuition," *Scientific American Mind* (June–July 2007).
37. Michael Michalko, *Thinkertoys: A Handbook of Business Creativity* (California: Ten Speed Press, 1991).
38. Ibid.
39. Keniche Ohmae, *The Mind of the Strategist* (New York: McGraw-Hill, 1982).
40. *The American Heritage Dictionary.*

41. Michael Gelb, *Discover Your Genius* (New York: HarperCollins, 2003).
42. Ibid.
43. Christensen, "Beyond the Innovator's Dilemma."
44. Baruch Fischhoff, "Visualizing Your Vulnerabilities," *Harvard Business Review* (May 2006).
45. Curtis Carlson and William Wilmot, *Innovation: The Five Disciplines for Creating What Customers Want* (New York: Crown Business, 2006).

Chapter 4

1. John McGee in David Faulkner and Andrew Campbell, eds., *The Oxford Handbook of Strategy* (New York: Oxford University Press, 2003).
2. Joseph Bower and Clark Gilbert, *From Resource Allocation to Strategy* (New York: Oxford University Press, 2005).
3. Al Neuharth, "Torre should take medicine like a man," *USA Today* (October 2007).
4. Aswath Damodaran, "Dealing with Intangibles: Valuing Brand Names, Flexibility and Patents," *Stern School of Business* (January 2006).
5. Robert Kaplan, "What to Ask the Person in the Mirror," *Harvard Business Review* (January 2007).
6. Richard Koch, *Smart Strategy* (New Hampshire: Capstone, 1999).
7. Massimo Garbuio et al., "How Companies Spend Their Money," *The McKinsey Quarterly* (May 2007).
8. Michael Beer, "Strategic Management as Organizational Learning," *Long Range Planning* 38 (2005).
9. Alan Deutschman, *Change or Die* (New York: Regan, 2007).
10. Michael Mankins, "Stop Wasting Valuable Time," *Harvard Business Review* (September 2004).
11. Bo Burlingham, *Small Giants* (New York: Portfolio, 2005).
12. Meg Whitman, "Bidding on Success," *Rotman Magazine* (Spring–Summer 2005).
13. Kevin Delaney, "Spreading Change," *Wall Street Journal* (November 18, 2006).

14. Peter Bedker et al., "How to Prune Trees," *USDA Forest Service* (1995).
15. James Hackett, "Preparing for the Perfect Product Launch," *Harvard Business Review* (April 2007).
16. Michael Porter, "What Is Strategy?" *Harvard Business Review* (November–December 1996).
17. John Byrne, "The Fast Company Interview: Jeff Immelt," *Fast Company* (July 2005).
18. Martin van Creveld, *The Art of War: War and Military Thought* (London: Cassell, 2000).

Chapter 5

1. Michael Mankins and Richard Steele, "Turning Great Strategy into Great Performance," *Harvard Business Review* (July–August 2005).
2. Michael Laff, "Execution Is Missing in Action," *T+D* (November 2006).
3. "Strategy Execution: Achieving Operational Excellence," *Economist Intelligence Unit* (November 2004).
4. Roger Martin, "How Successful Leaders Think," *Harvard Business Review* (June 2007).
5. Robert Kaplan and David Norton, "The Office of Strategy Management," *Harvard Business Review* (October 2005).
6. Fiona Czerniawska, "Executing Strategy: Lessons from Private Equity," *Strategy Magazine* (September 2007).
7. Ibid.
8. Joseph Bower and Clayton Christensen, "The Processes of Strategy Definition and Implementation," *Harvard Business School* (November 1, 1999).
9. Stephen Covey, *The 8th Habit* (New York: Free Press, 2004).
10. John Battle et al., "How to Succeed in 2004," *Business 2.0* (December 2003).
11. Kaplan and Norton, "The Office Strategy Management."
12. Jeff Bezos, "The Institutional Yes," *Harvard Business Review* (October 2007).
13. Covey, *The 8th Habit.*

Chapter 6

1. Jeanne Liedtka, "Linking Strategic Thinking with Strategic Planning," *Strategy & Leadership* 26, no. 4 (September–October 1998).
2. Vivienne Cox, "Cultivating Acumen at BP," *Strategy + Business* (Spring 2006).
3. William Joyce, Nitin Nohria, and Bruce Roberson, *What (Really) Works* (New York: HarperCollins, 2003).
4. Art Kleiner, "GE's Next Workout," *Strategy + Business* (Winter 2003).
5. Ibid.
6. Ibid.
7. F. William Barnett Jr. and Terrance Berland, "Strategic Thinking on the Front Lines," *The McKinsey Quarterly*, no. 2 (1999).
8. B.H. Liddell Hart, *Strategy* (New York: Meridian, 1954).
9. Richard and David O'Hallaron, *The Mission Primer: Four Steps to an Effective Mission Statement* (Virginia: Mission Incorporated, 1999).
10. Forest David and Fred David, "It's Time to Redraft Your Mission Statement," *Journal of Business Strategy*, no. 11 (January–February 2003).
11. Theodore Levitt, "Marketing Myopia," *Harvard Business Review* (September–October 1975).
12. Jeffrey Abrahams, *The Mission Statement Book* (California: Ten Speed Press, 1999).
13. Robert Greenleaf, *The Power of Servant Leadership* (California: Berrett-Koehler, 1998).
14. John Kotter, *Leading Change* (Boston: Harvard Business School Press, 1996).
15. Rich Horwath, *Sculpting Air: The Executive's Guide to Shaping Strategy* (Illinois: SC, 2006).
16. V. J. Bruce Harreld, "Dynamic Capabilities at IBM," *California Management Review* 49, no. 4 (Summer 2007).
17. Fiona Czerniawska, "Executing Strategy: Lessons from Private Equity," *Strategy Magazine* (September 2007).
18. Ibid.

19. Gerrard Hodgkinson et al., "The Role of Strategy Workshops in Strategy Development Processes," *Long Range Planning* 39 (2006).
20. Ibid.

Chapter 7

1. Phil Rosenzweig, "Misunderstanding the Nature of Company Performance: The Halo Effect and Other Business Delusions," *California Management Review* 49, no. 4 (Summer 2007).
2. Robert Rubin, *In an Uncertain World: Tough Choices from Wall Street to Washington* (New York: Random House, 2004).
3. Gregory Northcraft and Margaret Neale, "Experts, Amateurs and Real Estate: An Anchoring-and-Adjustment Perspective on Property Pricing Decisions," *Organizational Behavior and Human Decision Processes* 39 (1987).
4. Jeffrey Pfeffer and Robert Sutton, "Evidence-Based Management," *Harvard Business Review* (January 2006).
5. Giovanni Gavetti, "Strategy Formulation and Inertia," *Harvard Business School* (January 2005).
6. Max Bazerman and Dolly Chugh, "Decisions without Blinders," *Harvard Business Review* (January 2006).
7. Dan Lovallo and Daniel Kahneman, "Delusions of Success," *Harvard Business Review* (June 2003).
8. Scott Plous, *The Psychology of Judgment and Decision Making* (New York: McGraw-Hill, 1993).
9. Sam Savage, "The Flaw of Averages," *Harvard Business Review* (February 2002).
10. Irving Janis, *Groupthink: Psychological Studies of Policy Decisions and Fiascoes*, 2nd ed. (Boston: Houghton Mifflin, 1982).
11. Ibid.
12. Rosenzweig, "Misunderstanding."
13. Ibid.
14. Amos Tversky and Daniel Kahneman, "Judgment Under Uncertainty: Heuristics and Biases," *Science* (185): 1124–30.
15. Daniel Kahneman and Amos Tversky, "The Psychology of Preferences," *Scientific American* (1982): 160.

16. John Hammond, Ralph Keeney, and Howard Raiffa, "The Hidden Traps in Decision Making," *Harvard Business Review* (September–October 1998).

Chapter 8

1. *The American Heritage Dictionary of the English Language*, 4th ed. (Boston: Houghton Mifflin Company, 2000).
2. Michael Treacy and Fred Wiersema, *The Discipline of Market Leaders* (New York: Perseus Books, 1995).
3. Garry Kasparov, *How Life Imitates Chess* (New York: Bloomsbury, 2007).

ABOUT THE AUTHOR

Rich Horwath is the founder and president of the Strategic Thinking Institute, helping organizations achieve competitive advantage through strategic thinking. Rich is a former chief strategy officer and serves as a professor of strategy at the Lake Forest Graduate School of Management. He is the author of four books and more than fifty articles on strategic thinking. Rich is a highly sought-after speaker, blending the rare combination of high-level strategy content with a dynamic and engaging presentation style. He was recently ranked the #1 speaker out of 162 at the Society for Healthcare Strategy National Conference.

As an international thought leader in the area of strategic thinking, Rich has worked with Fortune 500 companies located in the United States, Europe, and Asia-Pacific. He helps leaders develop their strategic thinking skills and guides executive management teams through the strategy development process. His monthly publication, *Strategic Thinker*, is read by thousands of business leaders and academicians worldwide.

An innovator in the field of strategic thinking, Rich has designed a number of proprietary strategy tools to help executives grow their businesses. These tools include:

- Deep Dive Learning System™—a comprehensive blended learning approach to helping managers develop their strategic thinking skills through group workshops, practical application exercises, books, and one-on-one strategic counsel.

- StrategySphere System®—an online software program that contains forty strategic thinking models to generate business insights and set strategic direction.
- StrategyPrint®—a two-page blueprint containing the key insights and strategic action plan to achieve one's goals and objectives.
- Strategic Thinking Assessment™—a fifty-question diagnostic tool to determine a manager's baseline strategic thinking skills and to highlight areas for development.
- Strategy Vault—the premier online strategy resource center featuring hundreds of tools to strategically grow your business. The Strategy Vault provides users with 24/7 online access to articles, templates, assessments, instructional videos, software, journals and much more.

Rich earned an MBA with Distinction from the Kellstadt Graduate School of Business at DePaul University and has completed postgraduate courses in strategy at the University of Chicago Graduate School of Business and the Amos Tuck School of Business Administration at Dartmouth College. He resides in Barrington Hills, Illinois.

HOW CAN YOUR TEAM BECOME MORE STRATEGIC?

Help your management team sharpen their strategic thinking skills to achieve competitive advantage and profitably grow their business with the **Deep Dive Learning System**™—the most comprehensive strategic thinking learning system in the world. The Deep Dive Learning System will help your managers:

1. Apply the three disciplines of strategic thinking on a daily basis.
2. Create differentiated strategy to grow profits.
3. Improve strategic decision making to maximize productivity.
4. Write clear and effective strategies using the Strategy Formula.
5. Design a StrategyPrint to create a real-time strategic action plan.

The Deep Dive Learning System includes the following components:

- Strategic thinking assessments
- Group workshops

- Books and articles
- Deep Dive Workbook
- Deep Dive Logbook
- StrategySphere System software
- Individual strategic counsel

Looking for a high-content and dynamic keynote speaker for your next management off-site meeting or association conference? Rich was ranked the #1 speaker out of 162 at the Society for Healthcare Strategy National Conference. Formats include:

- 60- and 90-minute keynote speeches
- Half-day, full-day, and multiday workshops

Support your team's desire to excel and reach their full potential by contacting Rich today at (847) 756-4707 or rich@strategyskills.com

Get Better or Get Beaten

INDEX